*Across the Curriculum*

*with*
*Favorite Authors*

# Laura Ingalls Wilder

*Written by **Dona Herweck Rice***

*Illustrated by Agi Palinay*

***Teacher Created Materials, Inc.***

6421 Industry Way

Westminster, CA 92683

*©1998 Teacher Created Materials, Inc.*

Made in U.S.A.

**ISBN-1-55734-452-3**

# Table of Contents

# Laura Ingalls Wilder

(1867–1957)

Laura Elizabeth Ingalls was born in Pepin, Wisconsin, on February 7, 1867. Her father, Charles Philip Ingalls, was a farmer, carpenter, pioneer, and musician who instilled in Laura a love for music and for life that never left her. Her mother, Caroline Quiner Ingalls, was a homemaker and former teacher whose belief in education was instrumental in the love of learning that Laura demonstrated throughout her lifetime.

The early lessons of Laura's childhood were thrift, hard work, endurance, and a positive attitude. The family's daily task was survival. All of life's necessities they provided for themselves—hunting and growing their own food, knitting and sewing their own clothes, and building and furnishing their own homes. Self-sufficiency was key to their daily existence.

Laura was the second of five children. Mary Amelia was the first, born in Pepin in 1865. Carrie, or Caroline Celestia, arrived in Montgomery County, Kansas, in 1870. The only boy, Charles Frederick, was born in Walnut Grove, Minnesota, in 1875, but he died within a year, and there is no mention of him in the books. Finally, there was Grace Pearl, born in Burr Oak, Iowa, in 1877.

The family traveled frequently, moving from Pepin, Wisconsin, when Laura was two, to "Indian Territory" in Kansas. They moved back to their old farm in Pepin in 1871 and then on to Walnut Grove in 1874. The next relocation was for a year's stay in Burr Oak, Iowa, as caretakers of a hotel (the only childhood town not in the books), and then back to Walnut Grove in 1878. Due to depressed farming conditions, the family moved on with the railroad to become the first residents of a new town, De Smet, in Dakota Territory (now South Dakota) in 1879. It was there that Laura met Almanzo James Wilder, 10 years her senior, who became her husband on August 25, 1885.

Beginning at age 15, Laura taught a few terms of school around the De Smet area, and after marriage she joined with her new husband, whom she called *Manly*, in running their farm. There they had their only daughter, Rose, in December of 1886, and a son nearly three years later in August of 1889, although he lived for just a few weeks. During this time, Laura and Almanzo were both stricken with diphtheria, after which Almanzo overexerted himself and suffered what may have been a stroke or perhaps a case of polio. He never fully regained his health. They moved to Spring Valley, Minnesota,

# Laura Ingalls Wilder *(cont.)*

to stay with Almanzo's parents for a year and then on to Florida in 1891 for Almanzo to recover. However, the low altitude proved harmful to Laura, and they moved back to De Smet in 1892. There they worked and saved, earning the necessary money to make their final move. Their sights were set on "The Land of the Big Red Apple," the state of Missouri. Two years and $100 later gave them their start in the Ozarks of Mansfield, Missouri, and they began constructing their last home, Rocky Ridge Farm. Almanzo (an expert craftsman) and Laura designed and built the charming house themselves over a 15-year time span, and as testimony to their hard work, it stands today, serving as a tourist museum. Laura and Almanzo lived there until Almanzo died in 1949 at the age of 92, and Laura in 1957 at the age of 90. Their child, Rose, went on to become the celebrated world-traveling author, Rose Wilder Lane. Rose married for nine years but divorced, and her only child, a son, died at birth. She and her parents remained very close throughout their lifetimes.

Laura and Almanzo made quite a success out of their once little farm. Laura also went on to write for a farm paper, *The Missouri Ruralist,* and then, of course, in her sixties, with the support and editorial assistance of her daughter, she began to write the beloved *Little House on the Prairie* series, the first of which she wrote as a tribute to her father. It was published in 1932. It is believed that she was working on the final book, *The First Four Years,* when Almanzo died, and she chose never to complete it. The different style and abbreviated stories clearly suggest that it is a work in progress. Also, the book reflects none of Rose's hand, and therefore seems to be fully Laura's own. (Rose is noted for encouraging and probably editing her mother's books.) *On the Way Home,* Laura's diary account of the move to Mansfield, was forwarded and concluded by Rose and published in 1962. *West from Home*, a collection of letters written to Almanzo during a 1915 visit with Rose in San Francisco, was published by Roger Lea McBride (1929–1995), Rose's close friend, lawyer, and "adopted grandson," in 1974. William Anderson, a renowned scholar on the life of Laura Ingalls Wilder, published *A Little House Sampler* in 1988. It contains collected writings from both Laura and her daughter Rose. In 1991 Stephen W. Hines published an edited version of Laura's newspaper writings, entitled *Little House in the Ozarks: The Rediscovered Writings.*

There is one curious reaction to Laura's books that is worth note. Because the central character of the *Little House* books is the author herself, readers often assume all events and sequences in the nine books are true. Laura and Rose always upheld the accuracy of the events, and most documentation supports them. However, as mother and daughter also avowed, the sequences and some names are not actual, nor are all events from those years included. The books are fiction, written not as historical treatises, although they are based in fact. Laura's idea was to write an extended novel for children from her own childhood experiences. The series was intended for reader enjoyment and, quite honestly, for the author's financial gain.

Regardless of motive or historical accuracy, Laura Ingalls Wilder, through her wonderful books and inspiring character, left behind a legacy of experiences and lessons learned that have served and delighted millions worldwide. The daily joys and trials of pioneer life are made vivid for us all through her writings, as are the benefits of a productive, always-look-on-the-bright-side lifestyle. She is beloved even today, and her writings remain international treasures.

# Across the Curriculum with Laura Ingalls Wilder

The following pages are meant to give a sense of the author's place in history (1867–1957).* They will describe important events or experiences of her time in the fields of science, social studies, literature, history, art, music, sports, and entertainment. They will also provide lessons and activities coupled with those particular areas of the curriculum or, in the case of entertainment, an applicable field.

Additionally, students can research other people and events of significance during Mrs. Wilder's lifetime. The following time line shows the subjects from pages 6–13 of this book (in bold), with the inclusion of a random sampling of other worthwhile figures for study.

| | |
|---|---|
| 1830–1930 Mary Harris (Mother) Jones | 1870–1952 Maria Montessori |
| **1831–1890 Sitting Bull** | 1874–1963 Robert Frost |
| 1837–1901 Queen Victoria | 1879–1964 Lady Nancy Astor |
| 1838–1917 Queen Liliuokalani | 1881–1931 Anna Pavlova |
| 1840–1904 Chief Joseph | 1882–1945 Franklin D. Roosevelt |
| **1844–1926 Mary Cassatt** | **1887–1953 Jim Thorpe** |
| **1847–1931 Thomas Alva Edison** | 1889–1945 Adolf Hitler |
| **1848 Declaration of Sentiments at Seneca Falls** | **1889–1977 Charlie Chaplin** |
| 1852–1912 Emperor Mutsuhito | **1890–The Battle of Wounded Knee** |
| 1860–1951 W.K. Kellogg | **1891–1960 Zora Neale Hurston** |
| 1863–1947 Henry Ford | 1914–1918 World War I |
| 1866–1943 Beatrix Potter | **1920 The 19th Amendment** |
| 1867–1934 Marie Curie | 1920s The Harlem Renaissance |
| **1867–1957 Laura Ingalls Wilder** | 1929–1930s The Depression |
| **1868–1917 Scott Joplin** | 1939–1945 World War II |
| 1868–1918 Czar Nicholas II | 1950–1953 The Korean War |
| 1868–1963 W.E.B. DuBois | |

*(A time line entitled Ingalls-Wilder Family Time Reference can be purchased from five of the Laura Ingalls Wilder homesites listed on page 108. Compiled by Jane A. Williams, it lists important dates from the Little House novels and characters along with significant dates in American history throughout these same years. The time reference begins with the 1776 publication of the Declaration of Independence and the 1810 birth of Charles Ingalls' mother, and it concludes with the 1971 publication of The First Four Years.)

# The Author's Time in Science: The Age of Invention

Thomas Alva Edison was four days shy of his twentieth birthday when Laura Ingalls was born. Her life was filled with his fabulous inventions, like the phonograph and the electric light, as well as his perfection of other inventions like the typewriter and the telephone. Henry Ford suggested that the Age of Invention might more accurately be described as "The Age of Edison." In all, Edison patented 1,093 inventions.

Edison believed that genius was "one percent inspiration and two percent perspiration." What do you think he meant by this?

Edison also chose to work only on necessary inventions that met the "desperate needs of the world." Now here is your turn to follow Edison's example:

A local preschool is having trouble with their play equipment. They have a need for one slide (6' x 2' / 1.8m x .6m), one teeter-totter (6' x 1' / 1.8m x .3m), two swings (8' x 4' / 2.4m x 1.2m), and a jungle gym (5' x 5' / 1.5m x 1.5m). However, their current equipment is set up so that the children are always running into each other. They need a convenient arrangement that will allow eight children to play comfortably, but all of the equipment must be kept in the same corner of the play yard (20' x 15' / 6m x 4.5m). How would you design and arrange the play equipment? Remember, the most important things to consider in your planning are that the children are safe and that they can have fun. To construct a small scale model of your invention, use whatever items you like.

**Note to the teacher:** This is an excellent cooperative activity.

# The Author's Time in Social Studies: Women's Suffrage

Laura Ingalls was 53 when women in the United States were given the right to vote. The year was 1920, and the amendment that allowed them the vote was the 19th to the United States Constitution.

It was very important to Laura that she be an equal partner with her husband on the farm, but she was never a strong proponent of women's rights politically. Even so, she was aware of and celebrated changes for women, particularly having seen the important roles they played during World War I (1914–1918).

There were many women, however, who fought long and hard for concrete political reform just prior to and during Laura's time. Women like Lucretia Mott, Elizabeth Cady Stanton, Susan B. Anthony, and Lucy Stone spoke, petitioned, marched, lobbied, and sometimes even illegally voted in order to win support for women's suffrage. In 1848 at Seneca Falls, New York, the hometown of Elizabeth Cady Stanton, she and Lucretia Mott organized the first women's rights convention. Their Declaration of Sentiments was modeled after the Declaration of Independence, rephrasing it to read, for example, "We hold these truths to be self-evident, that all men and women are created equal . . . ."

Now is your opportunity to relive history with a broader cause—human rights. Write your own Declaration of Sentiments, listing in detail (in your own words) what the basic rights of all people are and why. You might begin by brainstorming your ideas, then organizing them in a web or outline, and finally drafting them into your declaration.

**Note to the teacher:** This activity can be done individually or in teams.

---

# The Author's Time in Literature: Zora Neale Hurston

When Laura Ingalls Wilder was in her fifties, a wave of potent and enlightening black literature rolled through New York City. The time was the 1920s, and the movement came to be known as *The Harlem Renaissance.* Among the many contributors to literature at the time, the author Zora Neale Hurston shines. Her work reflects a spirit of survival and, better, hope. A student of anthropology at Barnard College, Hurston is perhaps best known for her knowledge of black folk tales and lore, particularly from the United States and the Caribbean. She also became a prominent oral storyteller. Hurston's book *Mules and Men* is a collection of Florida and Louisiana folk tales and customs. The folk customs of Haiti and Jamaica are collected and described in a book called *Tell My Horse.* She also wrote novels and an autobiography called *Dust Tracks on a Road.*

Storytelling was also important in the Ingalls and Wilder households. As a tribute to both Zora Neale Hurston and Laura Ingalls Wilder, find a folk tale from your own ancestry, be it Native American, French, Mexican, Vietnamese, or other. Practice reciting this tale aloud, using emotion when you speak and facial expressions and gestures that reflect what you are saying. When you are comfortable and well practiced, share your tale with the class.

**Note to the teacher:** It may be beneficial to have a skilled storyteller visit your classroom and then have the class discuss what made that particular storyteller so good. You may also wish to model oral storytelling yourself.

# The Author's Time in History: The Battle of Wounded Knee

Ta-tan-ka Yo-tan-ka, or Sitting Bull, was 36 years old when Laura Ingalls Wilder was born, and he died when she was 23. Sitting Bull, along with other Sioux leaders, was present at the famous Battle of Little Big Horn on June 25, 1876, in which Colonel George Armstrong Custer and a detachment of his men died. Just two weeks after Sitting Bull's death, the last major battle between Native Americans and the U.S. government was fought in South Dakota, about 250 miles (400 kilometers) from Laura's hometown of De Smet. The fight is called the Battle of Wounded Knee.

Sitting Bull was a Sioux spiritual leader. He fought throughout his lifetime to maintain Indian lands. Yet the government did not often live up to their treaties and promises, and Sitting Bull and his fellow Sioux were repeatedly forced to give up their homes. Reservations became their homeland. The entire way of life for Indians changed dramatically during Sitting Bull's nearly 60 years.

By 1890 a new religion had arisen among the Indians of the reservations to keep their hopes alive. This religion involved a ghost dance, said to bring back the dead and the past way of life. Reservation officials became afraid, and policemen (Indian policemen) were dispatched to Sitting Bull's home. Sitting Bull resisted arrest, and before a crowd of 150 followers, he was shot in the back of the head by a policeman named Red Tomahawk. His 17-year-old son, Crowfoot, was also killed that day.

Hundreds of Indians fled to the Badlands of Dakota. The U.S. Cavalry caught up with them and brought them to Wounded Knee Creek. The next morning, while the soldiers were trying to disarm them, an Indian medicine man began to perform the ghost dance, and another pulled out a gun and shot wildly. The soldiers shot back with both guns and cannons. As a result, 200 Sioux (men, women, and children) and 64 soldiers died. The soldiers died mainly from their own bullets and flying shrapnel. The Indian wars, and in many ways the traditional Indian way of life, ended there on December 29, 1890.

Laura Ingalls Wilder was fascinated by Indians and their ways. She, like Sitting Bull, saw the Indian lifestyle change markedly. Today there seems to be a resurgence of interest in and support for Native American culture and beliefs. As a class, read *Brother Eagle, Sister Sky* by Susan Jeffers (Dial Books, 1991). Brainstorm some things that the class can do to preserve or rediscover the Native American lifestyle. Members of the class may wish to choose one of those things and pledge to carry it out. With the approval of their parents, they may make it a point of honor to live up to that pledge.

As a challenge, research the Battle of Wounded Knee and the events that led to it. Write down your perspective on the battle and the justice of the Indian's displacement.

# The Author's Time in Art: Mary Cassatt

Mary Cassatt was born in America in 1844, but she spent most of her life in France. Much of her art belongs to the great French impressionist movement. Perhaps Cassatt is best known for her typical subject matter—mothers and their young children. These subjects were not posed but were shown performing everyday activities, such as appears in her famous work *The Bath*.

Mary Cassatt was privileged not only with a great talent but also with the means to follow the career of her choice, although that was very rare for women of that time. Cassatt was independently wealthy, so unlike Laura Ingalls Wilder, she was able early in life to do things that women normally did not do. Namely, she became an artist and, although alone, moved far away from her home and family.

While Cassatt was a single woman, painting with the impressionists, Laura Ingalls Wilder was teaching school on the prairie, then marrying, raising her child, and running a farm with her husband. Wilder's work was traditional; Cassatt's was not.

If, today, you could choose your life's career and family circumstances, what would they be? Write a paragraph about these hopes and dreams. Set the paragraph aside while you create a work of art in honor of both Mary Cassatt and your own family. Draw, color, or paint a picture of yourself as a young child along with a special person who took care of you— perhaps your mother, father, or grandmother. When complete, attach your paragraph to the bottom of your own picture. If you would like, display your artwork and writing in the classroom.

---

# The Author's Time in Music: Scott Joplin

Scott Joplin, the son of a former slave, loved music all his life. Born in Texarkana, Texas, in 1868, he left home at 14 and traveled about the Mississippi Valley playing piano in saloons. He wound up at the Maple Leaf Club in Sedalia, Missouri. In Sedalia several of his compositions were published, including his most famous "Maple Leaf Rag." During his lifetime, Scott Joplin wrote or collaborated on over 60 pieces of music and became a leading composer of what is known as *ragtime*, or simply *rag*.

Ragtime was very popular in the United States around the turn of the century. The term *ragtime* is short for "ragged time," and it refers to a type of music that is sometimes irregularly accented (or syncopated) and then regularly accented. The music is very energetic. Ragtime started as improvisational, but composers like Joplin gave it a written form.

Though Joplin's life ended sadly and too soon (he died in 1917 in a mental hospital), he left a legacy of music that continues to delight and entertain. Joplin even received a special citation from the Advisory Board on the Pulitzer Prizes in the 1970s as a tribute to his contribution to music. In fact, the seventies saw a revival of interest in his music, in part because of a popular movie of the time called *The Sting*.

In the classroom, listen to a recording of Scott Joplin's ragtime music. While listening, close your eyes and see what pictures come into your head as you listen. When the music is finished, quickly write down all the things the music made you think and feel. In small groups of three or four, share one of those things. Were your thoughts and feelings similar or very different?

Music was important to Laura Ingalls Wilder, and she and her father often chose songs to accompany a particular experience. What experience do you think this music would represent well? As a class, brainstorm some appropriate places and situations to play Joplin's music.

---

# The Author's Time in Sports: Jim Thorpe

Jim Thorpe is widely considered one of the greatest athletes of all time. His talents ranged from football to baseball to track and field, and he was successful in all those areas. Born in Oklahoma in 1887, Thorpe, a Native American, began to show his athletic skill at the Carlisle Indian Industrial School. Because of him, the small school achieved national recognition.

In the 1912 Olympics, Thorpe became the first athlete to win both the pentathlon and decathlon. However, because he had earned a small salary as a baseball player prior to the 1912 games (which gave him professional status, not the amateur status required to compete in Olympic games) his medals were taken away about a month after he received them. In 1982 (29 years after Thorpe's death) the International Olympic Committee reconsidered and restored the medals.

A multi-talented athlete, Jim Thorpe played professional baseball for three major league teams (1913–1919) and football for seven teams (1915–1930). He became the first president of the American Professional Football Association (now the National Football League) and one of the first men admitted into the National Football Foundation's Hall of Fame (1951).

Due to Thorpe's fame and leadership in the world of athletics, Laura Ingalls Wilder would certainly have been aware of this incredible athlete. Today, although athletes show masterful skill in their fields, it is still quite rare for a single athlete to compete so successfully in several different sports.

As a tribute to Thorpe and as a means to show your own athletic skill (as well as to have a lot of fun), hold your own classroom pentathlon. The traditional events are the long jump, javelin throw, 200-meter run, discus throw, and 1,500-meter run. However, the whole class can choose which events to hold in your pentathlon. (**Note:** For obvious safety reasons, the javelin throw is not normally conducted in track and field meets until college level.) With the exception of the javelin throw, events can be the ones listed above, or they can be more colorful—like banana tossing or hopscotch. Most importantly, have fun!

# The Author's Time in Entertainment: Charlie Chaplin

Charles Spencer Chaplin was born in London in 1889. By 1910 he was touring the United States in variety halls and music clubs. In 1914 his character, "The Little Tramp," first appeared, and by 1919 his stardom and success were assured with the creation of the United Artists film corporation (which he founded with three fellow actors and directors). During the silent picture era, Chaplin was considered by many to be the funniest man in the world. The Little Tramp was adored, and many of his films were huge successes.

Chaplin was the ultimate perfectionist in his filmmaking, and it shows. His social life was not always peaceful, and his views were often controversial, but the contributions he made to film and entertainment cannot be disputed.

Movies came into existence in Laura Ingalls Wilder's lifetime. Though she, like the rest of the world, was intrigued by them, she was not a great fan of Charlie Chaplin himself. It seemed to be that way with Charlie Chaplin: there were those who were ardent admirers and those who very much disliked who he was. His life seemed naturally to strike up such controversy. However, though they may have disliked the man, generally speaking, people were taken with the image of The Little Tramp. Though he often seems sad, he is always loveable and endearing; and though poor and homeless, there is a jauntiness in his shuffle. Also, his trademark gloves, cane, and derby hat give the unmistakable air of one who has hope and the willingness to keep plugging away.

Laura Ingalls Wilder definitely had the spirit of endurance, perseverance, and a positive outlook. View one of Chaplin's Little Tramp films, like *The Kid* (1920) or *Modern Times* (1936). Next, in small groups of three or four, create an original character that you think represents all of these characteristics. The character can be realistic like Laura in Wilder's books or comical like the tramp. Describe in detailed notes how this character looks and behaves. Imagine the character at home, at work, at play, or wherever you might find him or her. When complete, share your character's name, description, and typical behaviors with the whole class. Are they all hopeful? Are they all survivors?

# Little House in the Big Woods

Written as a tribute to Charles Ingalls, this first novel in the nine-book set tells the story of the Ingalls family in the big woods near Pepin, Wisconsin. The character of Laura Ingalls is four to five years old here; therefore, the book is primarily an account of the time the family spent in the little house after having moved temporarily to Kansas. The Kansas period is told in the next book of the series, *Little House on the Prairie,* altering the factual series of events for literary purposes. Although based in fact, this book and all the others in the series are fiction.

*Little House in the Big Woods* is simply about a young girl's admiration for her father and the way of life he provided for his family. She tells fondly of their simple day-to-day living, hunting and preparing food, doing chores, playing, and telling stories. There is a sense of fulfillment in the house as the family prepares for winter months by stuffing their home with good things to eat and as the Ingallses share themselves with one another lovingly and supportively. Whether or not each of the events of the book is true to life, certainly the feelings conveyed are.

Beginning below and on the pages that follow, you will find individual chapter topics and activities. These may be done after each chapter, at the close of chapter groupings, or at the end of the novel. Also, they may be done individually, in small groups, or as a class. Determine what works best in your own classroom and pick only those items from the lists below that are appropriate for your students.

## Chapter Discussions and Activities

### Chapter 1: Little House in the Big Woods

1. The novel begins approximately in the year 1871. Describe the Ingalls home of that year as compared with your modern home. Think about such things as water, heat, light, cooking, food storage and preservation, household space, and communication with the outside world. Brainstorm some other elements to compare as well.

2. List the animals found in the big woods.

3. List the vegetables that the Ingalls family grows.

4. Compare how the Ingalls family got their food with how your family gets yours.

5. It was important to the Ingallses not to waste anything. List all the things they made with the butchered pig.

6. Why was the man foolish to cut two cat doors?

7. Use the chart on page 19 to keep track of all the food you eat in one day. Now, make a list of what you think Laura might have eaten in one day.

# Little House in the Big Woods *(cont.)*

## Chapter Discussions and Activities *(cont.)*

### Chapter 2: Winter Days and Winter Nights

1. Draw a picture of Jack Frost.

2. Write your own descriptive paragraph of a fictional character from nature (like Mother Nature, Father Time, the Sandman, the Grim Reaper, etc.). Use descriptive words that appeal to the senses—for example, ". . . Jack Frost was a little man all snowy white, wearing a glittering white pointed cap and soft white knee-boots made of deerskin." (*Little House in the Big Woods*)

3. Ma knows an old saying that tells her what chore to take care of on each day of the week. Which day would be your favorite? Your least favorite? Can you substitute something for each day of the week to make your own saying? Use page 20 to try this. Then, as a class, create a saying for things the class can do each day of the week. (You may wish to exclude Saturday and Sunday.) Also copy this saying onto page 20.

4. Make butter. Directions for the butter Ma makes (but without the churn) can be found on page 21.

5. Laura and Mary love the paper dolls that Ma makes for them. Use the patterns on page 22 to make your own. Draw on clothes and faces or make clothes to attach with shoulder tabs.

6. Practice being a "mad dog" like Pa. What other animals can you pantomime?

7. Learn about the cats of nature. What are their common characteristics? How are domestic cats, like Black Susan, different from wild cats?

### Chapter 3: The Long Rifle

1. What are the steps Pa takes to make bullets? to clean his rifle? to load his rifle?

2. Laura and Mary each have a special task to do when helping Pa load his rifle. Is there a task that you do regularly to help someone else do a necessary job? How do you feel about the help you give?

3. In the Ingalls household, it is very important to follow rules and the regular ways of doing things. Disobeying or changing the routine can be life-threatening for them. For example, what if Pa did not put his gun on the hooks over the door, and he needed it in an emergency? Or what if he reversed the steps in loading his gun? What are some of the rules in your family's house? List five of them. Next to each, write what you think is the reason for the rule. Does every rule have a reason? Do you think some rules should be changed? Do you think there are rules that should be added?

4. When Pa was nine, he was responsible for bringing the family's cows home every night. Do you think you are old enough to handle such a responsibility? How old do you think someone should be before becoming responsible for something like that?

# Little House in the Big Woods *(cont.)*

## Chapter Discussions and Activities *(cont.)*

### Chapter 4: Christmas

1. Using each of the five senses *except sight*, describe snow. Write only about how snow feels, tastes, sounds, and smells.

2. Wisconsin winters are beautiful. The white snow glimmers on treetops and rooftops; icicles hang everywhere. Find out about snow. Of what is snow made? Why does it snow?

3. Draw what you think Pa's Christmas bracket may have looked like.

4. Compare the food the Ingalls family had for their holiday dinner with a typical holiday meal at your house. Are there any similarities?

5. Laura was thrilled with her beautiful handmade Christmas gift, Charlotte. If you learn how to make a simple running stitch, you can make a rag doll like Charlotte, too. Pages 23–25 have patterns and directions for the doll's body and dress.

6. Laura and Mary didn't have many toys. Often, they needed to use their imaginations to find things to play with and new games to play. Cousin Alice introduces them to snow pictures. Brainstorm all the games you can play in and with snow.

### Chapter 5: Sundays

1. Why do you think the Ingalls family bathed only once a week?

2. Have a classroom contest to see who can sit perfectly still the longest. Do you think you could behave as quietly as Laura and Mary do on Sundays? What do you think of the way Laura's Grandpa had to spend his sabbath day?

3. Make a miniature sled like the one Grandpa and his brothers made. Use paper, cardboard, craft sticks, or whatever else you think will work to make a small sled.

4. One of the birthday traditions in Laura's family is birthday spankings. Does your family have any birthday traditions? What are they?

5. List the birthday gifts Laura receives.

6. Does something have to come wrapped up in a box to be a gift? Brainstorm all the different gift ideas you can.

### Chapter 6: Two Big Bears

1. Ma and Pa both face their fears in this chapter. Though confronted with a bear, Ma keeps her wits about her and gets herself and Laura safely back to the house. Pa faces down a "bear" because, as he says, "You see, I had to." For Ma and Pa, courage is doing what they have to do despite their fears.

   Have you ever had to face any fear to do what needed to be done? Write about it. Or write about a fear you might face and how you think you might handle it.

2. Pa is fooled by a tree stump that looks like a bear. Using black tempera paint, each student can make a random splotch on a piece of paper. In small groups, students can take turns holding up their splotches. Each student can suggest what each picture might be. How many different things do students see? Do any of the splotches look like bears?

   Alternatively, using a light projector, cast shadows of classroom objects on the wall. Do any of them appear to be anything else?

# Little House in the Big Woods *(cont.)*

## Chapter Discussions and Activities *(cont.)*

### Chapter 7: The Sugar Snow

1. Grandpa spends a lot of time whittling troughs. Draw what you think the troughs look like.
2. What steps are used in making maple sugar? Write to a modern maple sugar company and ask them to explain how maple sugar is made today. Compare it with Grandpa's technique.
3. What does "sugar snow" mean?
4. Why is Ma's delaine dress so special?
5. Ma hasn't worn her treasured delaine since Mary and Laura were born. What does that suggest about the life the Ingalls family leads?

### Chapter 8: Dance at Grandpa's

1. In what war do you think Uncle George has fought?
2. Uncle George enjoys the echo his bugle makes. What makes something echo?
3. List the things Laura loves about her grandparents' house.
4. Laura thinks that the dresses worn by Docia, Ruby, and her mother are the most beautiful she has ever seen. Describe the most beautiful or handsome outfit you can imagine.
5. Learn to square dance! What is meant by "grand right and left"? How about "doe see doe"?
6. Have a classroom dance-off, just like Grandma and Uncle George. Who can dance the longest and most energetically?
7. Has your family ever had a party like the one Grandma and Grandpa Ingalls have? If so, what was it like? How did you feel? Were you as excited as Laura?

### Chapter 9: Going to Town

1. From her fond description, it seems Laura really loves the coming of spring. What is spring like when it comes where you live?
2. What things do the Ingallses do in the spring that they don't do in the winter?
3. Why is going to town such an adventure for Laura and Mary?
4. Laura feels both excited and anxious when she goes to town for the first time. Can you remember a time in your life when you felt the same way? Describe it.
5. What are *galluses*?
6. Laura recalls the day in town as the most wonderful in her life. What has been your most wonderful day?

### Chapter 10: Summertime

1. What is a fair division of two cookies for three people?
2. Laura is often jealous of Mary. What are some of the reasons? Discuss feelings. Do they always make sense?
3. What chores do Laura and Mary do in the summertime?
4. Learn about the moon. Of what is it really made?
5. The Ingalls family is thrilled to have found such a supply of honey, but Laura is concerned about the bees. Learn how bees make honey and then decide if Laura has reason to be concerned.

# Little House in the Big Woods *(cont.)*

## Chapter Discussions and Activities *(cont.)*

### Chapter 11: Harvest

1. Draw chalk circles on the ground outside. Pretend these circles are tree stumps and jump from stump to stump. Who can jump farthest? How far can you jump?

2. Yellow jackets usually nest underground. When disturbed, workers will often sting repeatedly. Queens and males do not sting. Read about yellow jackets; then write a short play (from a yellow jacket's point of view) about the scene in the book.

3. Why does Pa call Charley a liar? Do you agree with Pa?

### Chapter 12: The Wonderful Machine

1. Ma makes beautiful hats from braided straw. If you can get some straw, try making a hat that way. If not, braid yarn and sew it together to make a hat—even a doll-sized one as Laura does.

2. The Big Woods are full of nuts in autumn. Gather nuts if they grow near you or get some from a market. What kind do you like best?

3. Practice math skills by sorting nuts by kind, color, and size.

4. Make johnny-cake! You will find a recipe on page 26.

5. What's the purpose of a threshing machine?

6. Do you agree with Pa that industry is a great thing? Brainstorm the pros and cons of industry.

### Chapter 13: The Deer in the Wood

1. The Ingalls family depends upon hunting for survival, so what reasons explain why Pa does not shoot the animals at the salt lick?

2. What do you think the last song Pa sings means? Today that same song is sung on New Year's Eve. Why do you think this is so?

3. Why is *now* important to Laura? Do you spend more time thinking about the past, the present, or the future?

## Culminations

1. In the Big Woods of Wisconsin, Laura enjoys dramatic and beautiful changes of season. What are her favorite things about each season? Are the seasons where you live like Laura's, or are they different? What are your favorite things?

2. What things do the Ingallses do for themselves (by hand) that you and your family do not have to do? What conveniences do you have that the Ingalls family does not have? Do you think the Ingalls family is happy with its way of life? Which do you prefer—life in the Big Woods in the 1860s and 70s or modern life in your hometown? What are the benefits of each?

3. Though there is no mention of school in the book, during this time the real Laura attended the Barry Corner School run by Miss Anna Barry. As a four-year-old, Laura was the youngest in the school. Use an encyclopedia to learn what a one-room schoolhouse of 1871 was like; then compare it with your school. What are the good things about each? What things don't you like?

4. Laura grows up in nature. Wild plants and animals are all around her. Even in the city, wildlife is nearby—insects and birds, in particular. What is the wildlife like where you live? How does it compare with life around the Ingalls' home?

# Daily Food Chart

Name _____ Date _____

## Today I ate . . .

Breakfast:


Lunch:


Dinner:


Snacks:

## On a day like today, I think Laura would have eaten . . .

Breakfast:


Lunch:


Dinner:


Snacks:

# All in a Day's Work

Name _____ Date _____

---

**Ma says . . .**

Wash on Monday,

Iron on Tuesday,

Mend on Wednesday,

Churn on Thursday,

Clean on Friday,

Bake on Saturday,

Rest on Sunday.

---

**I say . . .**

_____ on Monday,

_____ on Tuesday,

_____ on Wednesday,

_____ on Thursday,

_____ on Friday,

_____ on Saturday,

_____ on Sunday.

**The class says . . .**

_____ on Monday,

_____ on Tuesday,

_____ on Wednesday,

_____ on Thursday,

_____ on Friday,

_____ on Saturday,

_____ on Sunday.

---

# Making Butter

*At first the splashes of cream showed thick and smooth around the little hole. After a long time, they began to look grainy. Then Ma churned more slowly, and on the dash there began to appear tiny grains of yellow butter.*

You can make butter, too, and you do not need a churn and dash to do it. Just follow the simple directions below. Oh, there is one thing you will have in common with Ma—you are sure to need a rest, too!

## Ingredients:

- 3 cups (750 mL) heavy whipping cream, chilled
- ¼ cup (75 mL) milk
- 1 carrot
- salt

## Materials:

- grater
- saucepan
- 2-quart (2-liter) jar with tight lid
- 2-quart (2-liter) bowl
- strainer (fine)
- wooden spoon
- small dish or buttermold

## Directions:

Grate the carrot and heat it with the milk. Meanwhile, dip all materials but the grater and saucepan into boiling water to scald them, and then rinse them. Chill them in cold water. Strain the carrot from the milk into the jar and add the cream. Put the lid on the jar and shake it for about a minute. Open the lid once and refasten; then continue to shake the jar. After about 15 minutes, the liquid will become mushy and grainy. Strain it into the bowl; then dump the milk out of the bowl. Cover the butter in the bowl with cold water and stir. Strain off the water; repeat this washing process until the water is clear. Use the spoon to press the butter; this removes the liquid. After all liquid is gone, add a dash of salt and work it into the butter. Rinse again with cold water. Refrigerate your butter.

# Paper Doll Patterns

Draw faces and clothes on the paper dolls; then color them and cut them out. Or you can make paper clothes separately, being sure to leave tabs on the clothes to hold them onto the dolls. For fun, make clothes from Laura Ingalls' childhood and clothes that you or your friends might wear. Compare and contrast.

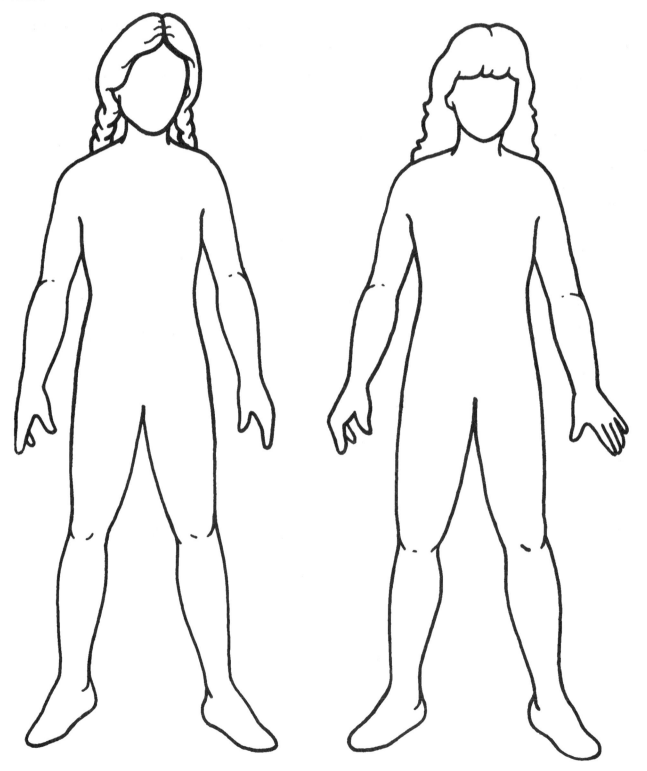

# Making a Rag Doll

Trace two body patterns from page 24 onto a thin muslin fabric or interfacing (but trace the face onto only one body). Lay the two body halves together, making sure the side that has the face is facing in. To stitch the two bodies together, use a running stitch along the dotted lines shown on the pattern, leaving one side of the body open for the filling to be stuffed in later.

When the two body halves are stitched together, turn the body right side out. Stuff the body with a cotton or polyester filling. Tuck the opening flaps in and stitch closed.

1. Make the doll's dress by tracing the pattern on page 25 onto whatever dress fabric is desired (the lighter the fabric, however, the easier it will be to trace the stitch marks).

2. Make two. Face the two dress halves together, outsides in.

3. Stitch with a running stitch as indicated on the patterns. Fold up the hem $\frac{1}{4}$" (.6 cm) and hem with a running stitch, as shown. Turn right side out. Sew lace (or use a fabric glue) around the arm and neck holes or stitch carefully with a small hem. Put the dress on the doll. Clip the neck down the back as much as necessary; and then stitch it closed, once on the doll.

Yarn can be braided, twisted, or fringed to create hair. Glue or sew it on. Add socks and shoes if desired.

4. Now your doll is complete!

# Rag Doll Body Pattern

See page 23 for directions.

# Rag Doll Dress Pattern

See page 23 for directions.

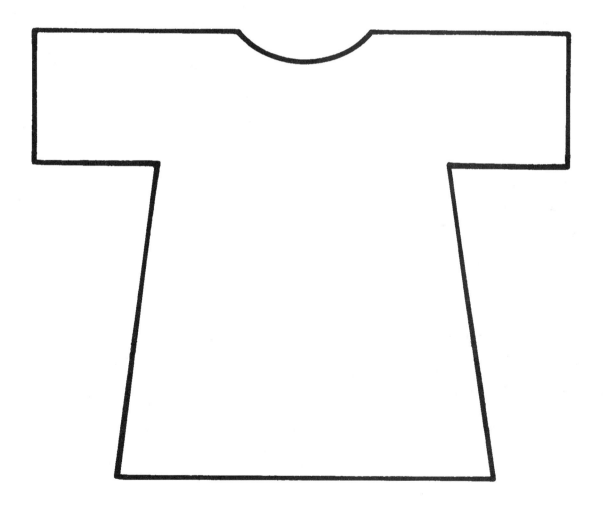

# Making Johnny-Cake

*Ma had heard some say it should be called journey-cake. She didn't know. It wouldn't be very good bread to take on a journey.*

But it is delicious bread to eat, as the Ingalls family knew well. Try it yourself! Here's a quick and simple recipe to follow.

## Ingredients:

- butter or margarine
- 1 cup (250 mL) white or yellow cornmeal
- 1 teaspoon (5 mL) salt
- 1 cup (250 mL) water
- ½ cup (125 mL) milk
- maple syrup or jam (optional)

## Materials:

- small saucepan
- griddle or frying pan
- medium mixing bowl
- mixing spoon
- spatula
- paper towel

## Directions:

Heat water in the saucepan until boiling. Meanwhile, grease the griddle or frying pan with a little butter or margarine (rub it on with a paper towel). Put the griddle on medium to low heat. Turn off the heat under the water when it boils. Mix the cornmeal and salt in the mixing bowl; add water, stirring until smooth. Add milk and stir. (The mixture will be thick.) Drop spoonfuls of batter onto the hot griddle, being careful not to let the batter for each johnny-cake touch. When the bottom side of each is golden brown, flip it over with the spatula and cook the other side. When that side is cooked to a golden brown, take the johnny-cake out and serve hot with butter, syrup, jam, or anything else you would like. Enjoy!

# Farmer Boy

While her first book was written as a tribute to her father, the second story Laura Ingalls Wilder undertook to tell was that of her husband, Almanzo James Wilder. The story takes place during approximately one year of young Almanzo's life. He is eight years old as the novel opens, celebrating life in ways that only a young boy can. Yet he longs for the confidence and trust of his father so that he might receive some additional adult responsibilities, especially pertaining to horses. Almanzo and Laura Wilder shared many things, including their love of horses, and the seeds of that love are more than evident here in the young boy.

Of particular interest in this novel are the differences apparent in the Wilder household as compared to the Ingalls' home. There is great affluence here and regular contact with the growing town of Malone. Although both were raised on farms, Almanzo and Laura experienced the differences of a rich farm meant for profit and a small farm meant for self-support.

Below and on the pages that follow, you will find individual chapter topics and activities. See page 14 for further explanation.

## Chapter Discussions and Activities

### Chapter 1: School Days

1. This book was first published in 1933. In what year does the novel take place?
2. What are your thoughts on Almanzo's school? Would you like to go there?
3. Name and give the ages of all the children in the Wilder family. (Mr. and Mrs. Wilder are named James and Angeline.)
4. At the time of this novel, the Wilders also had a daughter named Laura. What reasons do you think Laura Ingalls may have had for leaving Laura Wilder out of the book?
5. Find Malone, New York, on a map.

### Chapter 2: Winter Evening

1. List three ways in which Almanzo's school is different from yours. List three ways in which the two schools are similar.
2. How would you describe the financial standing of the Wilder family? (What is it like compared to the Ingalls family?)
3. List Almanzo's household chores. List yours. Would you like to trade any?
4. Make paper cutouts or draw on the board all of the food Almanzo eats for dinner. Do you think you could eat a meal like his?
5. Figure out how much the Wilders' supper would cost at today's prices. Use the worksheet on page 33.

### Chapter 3: Winter Night

1. What is *tallow*? What is a *pannikin?*
2. Do you think Almanzo is right about popcorn and milk? Try it and see.
3. Research the history of one of your favorite foods, like pizza, spaghetti, or hamburgers. Write or tell about it as Almanzo does with popcorn.

# *Farmer Boy* (cont.)

## Chapter Discussions and Activities (cont.)

**Chapter 4: Surprise**

1. There is terrible tension in the school as the students wait for the big boys to thrash their teacher. What do you feel about this? Do you think anything different might have been done? Does Mr. Corse do the right thing? Is Father Wilder right to help? Could this happen in your school today?

2. Why is this chapter called "Surprise"?

**Chapter 5: Birthday**

1. Why is Almanzo so pleased with his birthday gifts?

2. Do you think Father and Mother Wilder get time to rest? When?

3. Learn how a loom operates. Now weave a pattern. Follow the directions on pages 34–35.

**Chapter 6: Filling the Ice-House**

1. Why do the Wilders need to cut and store ice?

2. Storing ice is normal for Almanzo but rare today. Imagine something you do today being done by a machine in the future. Use page 36 to pick a topic and draw a machine that does the work described. On the back write a paragraph describing your machine.

**Chapter 7: Saturday Night**

1. Describe the steps Almanzo's family goes through to bathe.

2. What do you think of the bathing the Wilders do? Would you like to try their method yourself?

**Chapter 8: Sunday**

1. Do you celebrate a sabbath day at your house? What is it like? In what ways is it the same as or different from Almanzo's sabbath?

2. Name three things Almanzo wants that he does not have.

3. How far away is Malone from Almanzo's home? How long does it take the horses to get there? How long would it take today by car?

4. Brainstorm all the things you can buy that cost under 50 cents.

5. Do you think Almanzo would be gentle with horses if his father let him near them? Would he "ruin" them as his father fears?

6. At the end of the chapter, Almanzo is glad that chore time has come. Why?

**Chapter 9: Breaking the Calves**

1. Taste a carrot. Do you agree with Almanzo's description? How would you describe it?

2. After reading this chapter, list everything you know about breaking a calf.

3. Almanzo thinks that perhaps the calves were asking each other, "What happened?" From the calves' perspective, write a conversation about the events of this chapter.

**Chapter 10: The Turn of the Year**

1. Do you think Alice is right that the boys have all the fun in their home?

2. Try some wintergreen gum or candy. Do you love the taste as much as Almanzo and Alice do?

3. How do you get flavoring, maple sugar, and syrup in your home?

4. The Wilder children work hard to clean the family home. Which chore would you most enjoy? dislike? How much housecleaning do you do in comparison to Almanzo?

# *Farmer Boy* *(cont.)*

## Chapter Discussions and Activities *(cont.)*

### Chapter 11: Springtime

1. Read about colts and grown horses to find out more about them. Make a chart that compares and contrasts them.

2. Almanzo waits in frustration for the sun to come overhead. Study the movement of the sun by watching shadows. As a class, pick three evenly spaced times during the school day. At each time, go outside to the same place on the sidewalk or asphalt, have one student stand in position, and have another classmate trace his or her shadow. How is it different at each time? What makes it different?

3. Learn to whistle. Does anyone in the class know how to whistle through a blade of grass as Almanzo does?

4. Have a taste test to compare white bread with rye'n'injun bread (Boston brown bread). How are they alike? How are they different? Which do you prefer? Try making some of your own (most cookbooks have these standard bread recipes).

5. Almanzo and Alice have a discussion about the abilities of boys and girls. What do you think about their conversation? Have a class discussion about boys and girls and how they are alike and different.

6. Brainstorm as a class for all of the animal baby names you know. (Almanzo gives you three.) Look up those you do not know in the encyclopedia or another reference book. Then respond to Almanzo's suggestion that grown animals and animal babies are not the same thing.

### Chapter 12: Tin-Peddler

1. Build a peddler's cart using the pattern on page 37. Color it bright red and yellow, just as it is described in the book.

2. Nick Brown boasts that he can tell more stories and sing more songs than any other man or group of men. How many stories and songs do you know? In groups of three or four, brainstorm two lists: "Stories" and "Songs." Your teacher will give you about 10 minutes to do this. Afterwards, compare with the other groups. Which group is most like Nick Brown?

3. Find out about tin and how it is shaped into tools and toys. Are the methods used today the same as the methods of Almanzo's time?

### Chapter 13: The Strange Dog

1. In this chapter, Father Wilder cuts a deal with the horse trader. In the last chapter, Mother Wilder does the same with the tin-peddler. What tactics do they both use in order to get what they want?

2. Where would you hide something in order to keep it safe? If you needed to find something someone else had hidden, where would you look? Do you think any of those places are good hiding places?

3. Has anyone or anything ever saved you from trouble?

### Chapter 14: Sheep-Shearing

1. Research kinds of sheep. Compare and contrast them.

2. Almanzo plays a good joke in this chapter. Have you ever played a joke like Almanzo does? If so, what happened?

3. What reactions do you think people normally have when they are fooled or when someone else got the better of them?

# Farmer Boy (cont.)

## Chapter Discussions and Activities (cont.)

**Chapter 15: Cold Snap**

1. Why is the cold snap a problem for the Wilders?
2. Find out why the Wilders must pour water on the corn plants to save the corn from freezing.

**Chapter 16: Independence Day**

1. Compare and contrast your Independence Day celebrations with those of Almanzo.
2. List all the things you can remember that happen on Almanzo's Fourth of July.
3. Research "The Star-Spangled Banner." When was it written? When was it adopted as the national anthem?
4. Discuss Mr. Wilder's point of view about the making of America. As part of your discussion, consider the people already inhabiting the United States of America. Were they rightfully removed and relocated? Were the citizens of the United States justified in taking land across the nation? Were there any wrongs or injustices done? Who is right? Think about such a thing happening today, for example, in Canada or Australia. Are such actions justifiable?

**Chapter 17: Summer-Time**

1. Illustrate the process of milk-feeding a pumpkin, based on the description in the book.
2. Almanzo fishes in the rain. What do you do when it rains?
3. For fun, Almanzo goes berrying. What do you do for fun? Does Almanzo's berry-picking day sound like fun to you?

**Chapter 18: Keeping House**

1. List Mother Wilder's rules for her children while she is away at Uncle Andrew's.
2. List things you would do if your parents were away for a week.
3. Have a taffy pull. You can find a recipe for making the candy in a confectioner's cookbook.
4. Do you have a formal room in your house (like the Wilder parlor), or does someone you know have one? Describe it. What are the rules for such a room?
5. Describe Almanzo's feelings when he runs from Eliza Jane and climbs into the haymow. Have you ever done anything that makes you feel the way Almanzo does at this time? Tell about it.
6. Eliza Jane patches the wallpaper that Almanzo marked, and she does not tell Mother and Father Wilder. Why do you think Eliza Jane does this? How do you feel about what she does? Has anyone ever done anything like that for you?

**Chapter 19: Early Harvest**

1. Define the following as they are used in *Farmer Boy: scythe, swathe, windrow, cradle, sheaf, reaper, maul, shock,* and *whetting stone.*
2. Make and drink egg nog.
3. Make butter. (See page 21.)

**Chapter 20: Late Harvest**

1. Find out proper procedures for doctoring burns such as Almanzo gets from the exploding potato.
2. Explain how your family stores and uses two of the following: pumpkins, apples, onions, red peppers, carrots, and potatoes.

# Farmer Boy *(cont.)*

## Chapter Discussions and Activities *(cont.)*

**Chapter 21: County Fair**

1. What do you think of Father Wilder's advice, "Never bet your money on another man's game"? Explain your response.

2. Research one of the following breeds and describe/explain it for the class:
   - Horses: *Morgan, Belgian, mule*
   - Cows: *Guernsey, Jersey, Devon, Durham*
   - Pig: *Chester White, Berkshire*
   - Sheep: *Cotswold, Merino* (See chapter 14 activities and questions.)

3. Father Wilder is normally very thrifty. So why does he tell Almanzo that it is all right to bet on horse races?

4. Look in the encyclopedia under Track and Field to find the current record for running the mile. How does it compare to the Indian's time? What do you think of this story?

5. Have a class race across the playground or run individually and time yourselves.

6. Have you ever entered a contest? Describe your feelings. Were they anything like Almanzo's?

7. "Three days of it were too much." What does Almanzo mean by this? Have you ever had a similar feeling? Explain.

**Chapter 22: Fall of the Year**

1. Almanzo and Alice play "wild Indian." This is a stereotypical term, one common for the time but perhaps inappropriate for today. Why is that?

2. Have a class discussion about "butchering-time." How does everyone feel about it? Discuss the pros and cons.

3. Make candles. Page 38 will show you how.

**Chapter 23: Cobbler**

1. Learn about the history of shoes and how they vary over time and across the world.

**Chapter 24: The Little Bobsled**

1. Father Wilder explains to Almanzo that no two things are alike. Write your thoughts about this idea.

2. Based on the description in the book, draw the bobsled. Compare your illustration to the one in the book. Are they both accurate?

**Chapter 25: Threshing**

1. What is a *flail*? Define it and draw it.

2. Almanzo wants to tell the animals "You can depend on me." How do you think he feels in thinking this?

# Farmer Boy (cont.)

## Chapter Discussions and Activities (cont.)

### Chapter 26: Christmas

1. The Wilder Christmas celebration is quite an extravaganza of food and fun. What is the best celebration you have ever enjoyed? Write about it as though it were part of a story and include yourself as the main character.

### Chapter 27: Wood-Hauling

1. Why do you think Father Wilder drives on when he sees Almanzo struggling in the snow the first time the steers go off the road?

2. How does Almanzo's schooling compare to yours? (See chapter 2 questions.)

3. Would schooling such as Almanzo experiences be adequate for a person in today's world? Explain your answer.

### Chapter 28: Mr. Thompson's Pocketbook

1. Father Wilder uses some mental detective work to figure out who owns the billfold Almanzo finds. In small groups, make up a mystery for another group to solve, just like the one about the billfold. When you have completed your work, exchange mysteries with another group; then solve the one the group gives to you.

2. Do you think Almanzo deserves the two hundred dollars? Why or why not?

### Chapter 29: Farmer Boy

1. In this chapter, Almanzo thinks over all the things he likes to do. What do you enjoy doing? Make a list of the things you like to do.

2. What is Almanzo's decision? Does he want to make wagons, or does he want to be a farmer?

3. Why is Almanzo reluctant to tell his father what he wants?

4. Tell about an important decision you have had to make in your life.

## Culminations

1. As farmers, the Wilders grow many vegetables. On the school grounds, make a vegetable garden. Care for it diligently. When the vegetables are grown, have a class party to enjoy them.

2. Bring in traditional American foods to eat and enjoy, similar to the kinds that Almanzo feasts upon throughout the book.

3. Make a class cookbook of recipes to go along with the many foods in *Farmer Boy*.

4. Write and illustrate a class book about horses. Tell about their history, show the different breeds, explain their natures, and tell how people have used them throughout time.

5. As a class, list all the things grown and produced on the Wilder farm. Across from each item, write the ways in which you as a class get each of these products today.

6. Make an illustrated dictionary of all the farm equipment used in *Farmer Boy*.

# Supper Tab

Everything the Wilders eat, they grow and harvest themselves. The costs involved are those of their time and labor. Most people today, however, do not grow all their own food. They shop at grocery stores, produce stands, and delicatessens in order to get food for their meals. To find out what the Wilder family meal would cost today, find the prices for each of the foods listed below and figure out how much is needed for a family of six with one visitor. Total the cost at the bottom.

| Food | Quantity | Cost |
|---|---|---|
| Cheddar cheese | | |
| Jack cheese | | |
| Cottage cheese | | |
| Strawberry jam | | |
| Grape jelly | | |
| Plum preserves | | |
| Milk | | |
| Baked beans | | |
| Salt pork (or bacon) | | |
| Ham | | |
| Potatoes | | |
| Gravy | | |
| Bread | | |
| Butter | | |
| Turnips | | |
| Pumpkin | | |
| Pickles | | |
| Pumpkin pie | | |
| Tea | | |
| **Total Cost:** | | |

**Question:** Do you think that many people today eat regular meals like this? Why or why not?

# Weaving

Mother Wilder weaves most of the fabric the family uses for clothes. Here is a simple way to learn about the process of weaving and even to make something yourself.

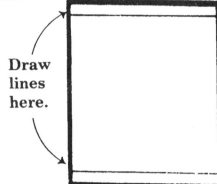

**Draw lines here.**

## Materials:

- smooth cardboard
- ruler or straight edge
- pencil
- scissors
- yarn (at least 2 colors)
- popsicle stick (with a hole drilled near one end)

## Directions:

1. Cut the cardboard into a rectangle. The length should be 1" (3 cm) longer than the width. The general size is up to you. (The bigger it is, the more weaving you will need to do.)

2. Draw a line across the top and bottom of the length ends, ¹/₂" (1.5 cm) in from the edge.

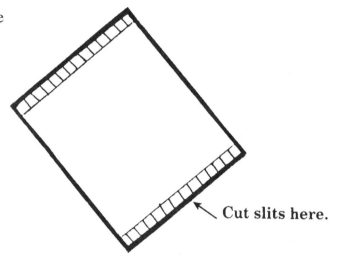

**Cut slits here.**

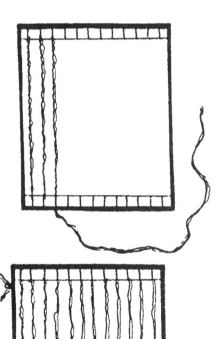

3. Carefully cut slits up to the lines in each length end. The slits should be ¹/₄" (1 cm) apart. Be sure that you have the same number of slits at both the top and the bottom of your loom, directly across from each other. You now have a loom.

4. Knot a long piece of yarn at the end. Put the knot behind the top left slit.

5. Bring the yarn straight down to the bottom left slit. Wrap it under the flap of the cardboard and come up through the second bottom slit from the left.

6. Bring the yarn straight up to the second top slit from the left. Go under and come up in the third slit.

7. Repeat this until you have come to the last slit. Knot the yarn behind it. These yarn strands are called the *warp*. Be sure they are not too tight. Otherwise your loom will bend.

# Weaving *(cont.)*

8. With the other color yarn, thread the popsicle stick with the hole drilled in one end. Make the length of yarn such that you can easily work with it. If it is too short, you can always tie more yarn to it as you go.

9. Weave across the warp, going over first, then under. The yarn you are weaving with now makes the *weft*. Tie the weft strand where you began into a knot around the first warp strand.

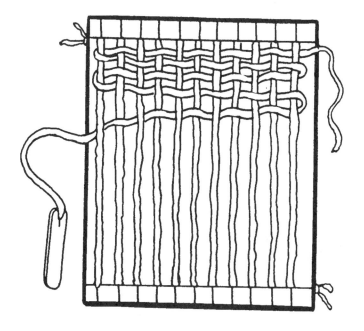

10. When you are ready to go back across the warp for the second row of the weft, go over the strands you went under before, and under the strands you went over. Push the weft strands closely together.

11. Experiment with different colors of yarn for the weft if you would like. You will be able to create many interesting designs.

12. Completely fill the loom with the weft. Knot the end of the yarn under the last weave.

13. Carefully slip your weaving off your cardboard loom.

14. Use the woven square for a potholder, place mat, or doll rug/blanket. You may even want to stitch squares together to create larger things such as blankets and rugs.

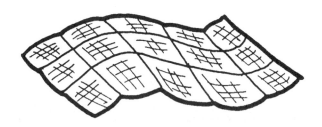

# My Invention

Imagine something common for you to do today being done only by a machine in the future. Pick a topic from the list below (or think of one of your own); then draw a machine that does the work described. On the back of the paper, write a paragraph description of your machine.

- brushing teeth
- dusting
- feeding the dog
- setting the table

- combing hair
- driving a car
- washing windows

- making a bed
- pulling weeds
- cooking dinner

# Peddler's Cart

Color, cut out, fold, and glue this peddler's cart. (Cut on the heavy lines and fold on the dotted lines.) Make a horse out of paper or clay and attach it to the front of the cart with yarn and sticks for reins and harness, if desired.

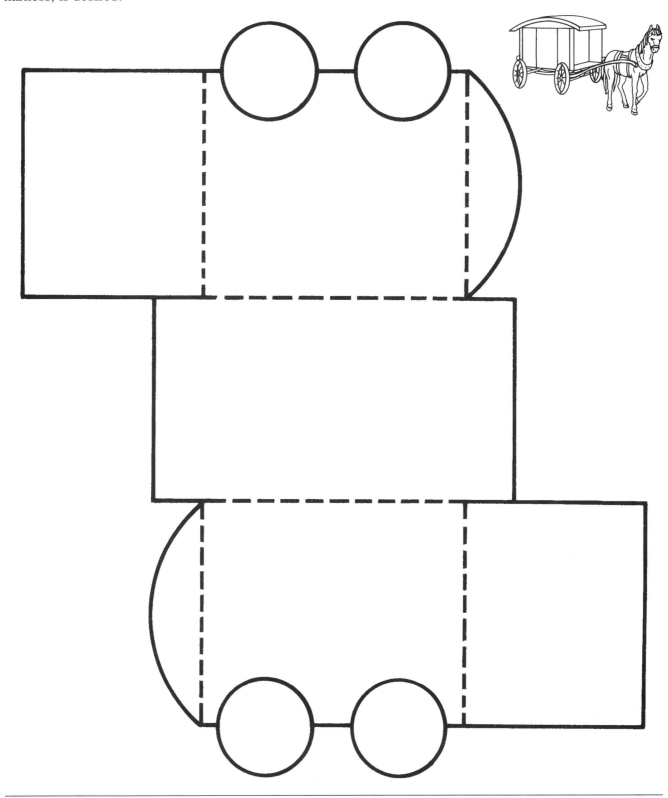

# Candle Making

## Materials:

- paraffin
- 8" (21 cm) candlewick (per candle)
- dowel or rod for drying candles
- large empty can (11- or 12-ounce coffee can)
- large saucepan (large enough for the can to be placed inside without the water overflowing)
- water

## Directions:

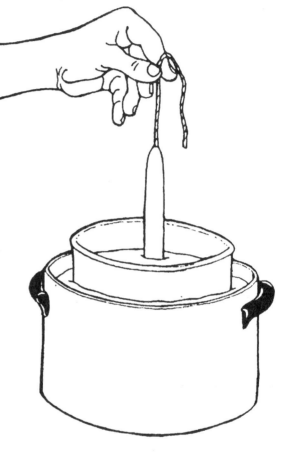

1. Fill the saucepan with 2" to 3" (5 cm to 8 cm) water.

2. Turn heat on low.

3. Put the paraffin in the can and the can in the water. Let the paraffin melt slowly.

   **Caution:** *Paraffin is flammable when too hot; keep the temperature low. Also, hot wax will burn your skin. This should be done only by an adult or with adult supervision.*

4. Add more paraffin if necessary to reach a depth of 4 inches (10 cm).

5. When the paraffin is melted to a liquid wax, lower the wick into the wax until the end reaches the bottom of the can (4"/10cm).

6. Slowly pull up the wick so that the candle is completely out of the wax.

7. Hold the candle up for a moment to cool and become solid, and then lower it again.

8. Repeat until the candle is the desired thickness.

9. Use the extra 4 inches of wick to hang the candle from the dowel to cool completely.

10. Cut the string about ¼" to ½" (.5 cm to 1 cm) above the top of the candle. Your candle is now complete!

---

**Note:** To make a simple candleholder, cut an X slightly smaller than the base of the candle into the plastic top of an old coffee can. Push the candle base through so that the candle is firmly in place. Light the wick and enjoy.

---

# Little House on the Prairie

The third book in the Little House series, *Little House on the Prairie,* continues Laura Ingalls' story from the time of *Little House in the Big Woods.* In reality, the events of this book happened before the events of *Big Woods;* however, Laura chose to tell them here. The book opens with the Ingalls family—Charles, Caroline, Mary, Laura, and Carrie—leaving their relatives in the woods of Wisconsin and traveling southwest across Minnesota, Iowa, and Missouri, and finally settling in the prairies of Kansas.

As they travel, details of pioneer life are clearly outlined, thereby enfolding the reader in an important part of American history. We journey with the Ingalls family, and step by step build their homestead with them on the fertile prairie land near the Verdigris River. We see how their home is made, how they work the land, how the children play, and how a family survives in a new, unfamiliar, and untamed environment.

Indians, as Laura knew them, play an integral part in the story; however, Laura's mother views the Indians as savage, and their behaviors, as seen through Laura's eyes under the guardianship of her mother, are sometimes shown as brutal and unfeeling. Additional study and discussion of Native Americans and their role in this book would certainly be fitting.

The Ingalls family endures many hardships and many joys on the prairie, but after a year's stay, they are forced to move onward. The novel closes with the family once more en route in their covered wagon, their next adventures before them somewhere across the sea of prairie grasses.

Below and on the pages that follow, you will find individual chapter topics and activities. See page 14 for further explanation.

## Chapter Discussions and Activities

### Chapter 1: Going West

1. What are some of the reasons Pa wants to leave the Big Woods?

2. The Ingalls family leaves their home in winter so that they can cross the Mississippi River while it is still covered in thick ice. What are some ways in which seasons and weather conditions affect travel today?

3. Draw a picture of Laura or Mary as they might have appeared in their travel clothes on the first day of their journey.

4. The Ingalls family is able to fit everything they need in one covered wagon. If your family had only one covered wagon and you were going to move, what do you think your family might pack? (See page 45.)

5. Laura writes of the little house as though it were a person and able to see them leave. How do you think your house might feel if you were to move away?

6. Imagine you are Laura looking across the frozen lake with the tracks leading to some unknown spot. Draw a picture of what you might find on the other end of the tracks. (See page 46.)

7. Research mustangs to find out about that breed of horses.

# Little House on the Prairie (cont.)

## Chapter Discussions and Activities (cont.)

### Chapter 2: Crossing the Creek

1. When the creek crossing becomes dangerous, Laura sits straight up to watch while Mary hides in the blankets. In a frightening situation, how are you most likely to behave—like Laura or Mary?

2. Have you ever lost a pet? Describe how you felt.

### Chapter 3: Camp on the High Prairie

1. Do some research to find out about wolves and their behaviors. Compare wolves and dogs.

### Chapter 4: Prairie Day

1. As a class, wash some clothes or bits of fabric as Ma does.

2. Draw a picture of the gophers as they appear to Mary and Laura. Research about gophers.

### Chapter 5: The House on the Prairie

1. Locate the Verdigris River and the town of Independence on a map. (Laura writes that her homestead is 40 miles from Independence; however, it was actually about 15 miles.)

2. Laura describes feeling small on the prairie. Have you ever felt that way? Describe it.

3. Discuss American Indians of the time. How are Laura's perceptions different from reality?

4. Build a model log house. (See page 47.) Draw the skids as you envision them.

5. Sing "Old Dan Tucker." Listen to birds or recordings of bird songs. Imitate them.

### Chapter 6: Moving In

1. Construct furniture for a log cabin, using your imagination or the patterns on pages 48, 49, and 50.

2. Write to relatives far away. Describe what life is like for you. Ask them to write back.

3. Make a list of songs about the moon or mentioning the moon.

### Chapter 7: The Wolf-Pack

1. Were you ever scared as Laura is when the wolves surround her home? Describe your experience.

### Chapter 8: Two Stout Doors

1. Draw models of the doors Pa builds, just as described here.

### Chapter 9: A Fire on the Hearth

1. List the creatures Laura and Mary see at the creek. Find a picture or illustration of at least one.

2. Using pebbles and soft, wet clay, construct a chimney such as Pa builds from stones and mud. Prop it against a wall of thick cardboard or use the log cabin you built.

3. In the Ingalls family, the china shepherdess is a special heirloom. Do you have any heirlooms in your family? Describe one.

4. In this chapter, the Ingalls family lives in a fully functioning house after weeks of temporary shelter. Imagine living that way today. What would it be like for your family? Could you manage living on a dirt floor and cooking in a fireplace? How would you like to fetch all your water from a nearby creek? Could you sleep on beds stuffed with straw on a dirt floor?

# Little House on the Prairie *(cont.)*

## Chapter Discussions and Activities *(cont.)*

### Chapter 10: A Roof and a Floor

1. Laura and Mary's day is filled with many things. List everything they do in their day. Then, list everything you do in yours on a nonschool day. How do they compare?

2. The gray rabbit stands perfectly still. Who in your class can stand still the longest? Have a contest to find out.

3. If a sunbonnet is available, put one on. Do you see what Laura means when she says it blocks her vision? Would you wear it to protect your skin, or would you let it hang down your back?

4. Have you ever swung an ax to chop wood? Describe it for classmates. Discuss how it might feel to chop and smooth enough logs for a roof and a floor such as Pa builds.

### Chapter 11: Indians in the House

1. Indians come into the Ingalls' home in this chapter. They are depicted as wild men who are to be feared and pacified. This portrayal merits a full class discussion, particularly on such topics as fear and racism. The students should also be told the full story as to why the Ingalls may have had this perspective. It would be beneficial to read other portrayals of American Indians that show them more fully, such as *Sign of the Beaver* by Elizabeth George Speare. Remind the students that the portrayal in this book is meant to be the perspective of a little girl.

### Chapter 12: Fresh Water to Drink

1. Draw or construct the bedstead as it is described in this chapter.

2. Make a straw tick. Divide into small groups. Each group will start with an old pillowcase and fill it with clean, dry straw or grass. You can purchase this from a craft store or a feed shop or simply have the students collect it from their home lawn mowers and dry the grass at school. Sew the open end of each pillowcase closed. Fluff out the pillows. Lay the pillows down end to end so that, together, they make a straw tick. Let the children take turns lying on the tick in order to experience what Laura and her family slept on each night. (Alternately, you can open the closed end of each pillow case and sew the cases together or sew two old twin sheets and stuff them as a whole-class project.)

3. Find a picture of a *windlass*. How does it work?

4. Locate illustrations that show interiors of the earth, depicting the water table in relationship to the surface. A local state water agency is likely to have maps showing the water table in your area.

5. Research the science behind the gas in the well and the removal of the gas with the gun powder explosion.

### Chapter 13: Texas Longhorns

1. Learn and sing some cowboy songs.

2. Research to learn more about cowboys of the late 1800s.

3. Laura writes that Pa laughs like "great bells ringing." Listen to the laughter of three different people—either those you know, hear in public, see on television, or hear on the radio. Describe each laugh, using a simile such as Laura uses.

4. Pa builds the cow milking pen. Draw a picture of that pen as you envision it.

# Little House on the Prairie (cont.)

## Chapter Discussions and Activities (cont.)

**Chapter 14: Indian Camp**

1. In this chapter, Laura describes a very hot day and its effects on her senses. Reread those parts and then write your own description of a very hot day. Share your descriptions with the class. As a challenge, describe a very cold day.

2. Make beads and necklaces. You can paint beads purchased at a craft store, mold them from modeling clay and sun-dry them, or paint Styrofoam popcorn pieces. String them with a needle and thread or fishing line. Give the necklace to someone you love.

3. As a class, look around outside and attempt to "read" the signs of recent events as Pa and the girls do at the Indian campsite. **Note:** In reality, Carrie was born on this day or one like it. Pa took Laura and Mary out for a day at an Indian camp, and when they returned, they found their little sister had been born. Laura was actually about three and one-half at the time.

**Chapter 15: Fever 'n' Ague**

1. Research malaria, its cause and its cure.

2. Dr. George A. Tann really lived (1825–1909) and tended sick Indians and settlers. Discuss Laura's first fear of Dr. Tann (fear of the unfamiliar). Relate this to the family fear of Indians.

**Chapter 16: Fire in the Chimney**

1. In her fear, Laura does the nearly impossible by pulling Mary and Carrie away from the fire. Has fear ever helped you to do something extraordinary? How about someone you know?

**Chapter 17: Pa Goes to Town**

1. What do you think of Mrs. Scott's arguments about the land belonging to people who will farm it?

**Chapter 18: The Tall Indian**

1. This is an important chapter about American Indians, settlers, and land rights. Continue your class discussion on these topics.

2. Research the Osage, especially about the time of these events.

**Chapter 19: Mr. Edwards Meets Santa Claus**

1. Sew quilt blocks. Make a class quilt.

2. Make paper dolls from wrapping paper.

3. Describe your happiest Christmas (or another special day).

4. Do you know a story of someone's selfless act of kindness? What happened? Write it as a story to share with the class just as Mr. Edwards shares his story with Laura and Mary.

5. Laura and Mary are thrilled with the gifts they receive in their stockings. To the girls, they are a treasure trove. What could you find in a stocking to make you as joyful as they are?

**Chapter 20: A Scream in the Night**

1. Play Hide the Thimble, Bean Porridge Hot, and Cat's Cradle. To play Hide the Thimble, "It" hides a thimble somewhere in the room while the others close their eyes. Then It calls out, "Thimble, thimble, find the thimble." The others look. The one who finds the thimble is the next It. Bean Porridge Hot is played as described in chapter 20. A Cat's Cradle can be found on page 51.

2. In this chapter, an Indian has killed a panther, and Laura believes it was to protect his children. How is the portrayal of Indians broadened by this encounter?

# Little House on the Prairie (cont.)

## Chapter Discussions and Activities (cont.)

### Chapter 21: Indian Jamboree

1. Play hopscotch.
2. Laura describes the sounds of the Indian language—speaking and chanting. Listen to recordings of various languages or to people actually speaking them. Describe how each language sounds to you, just as Laura describes one here.
3. Crackers and sour pickles are a real treat to the Ingalls family. What might your parent bring home that is a special treat for your family?
4. Do you think the Indians are justified in wanting the settlers to move away? Are the settlers justified in wanting the Indians to move west?

### Chapter 22: Prairie Fire

1. Why do Pa and Ma plow the furrow and start a fire of their own?

### Chapter 23: Indian War-Cry

1. The Ingalls family is living with a great deal of tension. Can you think of any modern-day situations in which people live under a threat such as the Ingalls family is living with?
2. What is a *stockade*? Describe it and its purpose. Draw a model sketch of one.
3. Why do you think Pa does not want to show that he is afraid?
4. What do you think Laura fears from the Indians?
5. Research to find what American Indian tribes were in the area at this time.
6. Why do you think the Indians wished to kill the white settlers?
7. Why do you think the Osages disagreed with the other Indians?
8. Soldat du Chene is credited with being a great soldier and a great leader. He was very influential with a great many people. What other people from history can you name who were or are influential in this same way?
9. Have you ever been able to influence other people to do what you thought was right? How? What happened?
10. Have you ever missed a night of sleep or more? If so, describe how that kind of tiredness feels.

### Chapter 24: Indians Ride Away

1. Throughout the book, Laura repeatedly calls the Indians "savages" and "wild men." What do you think of this?
2. Laura writes that Soldat du Chene's face will always be "proud" and "still." "Only the eyes were alive" in his face. Do you think this is true? Do you imagine a person might go through each and every day without facial expression?
3. Why do you think the Ingalls family believes it is shameful for "big girls" to cry?
4. Why do you think Laura cries out in longing for the Indian baby? Does she think of it as a doll, or what is it that she is really calling for?
5. In the beginning of this book, we see how the Ingalls family operates when they relocate. How does this compare to how the Osages relocate? Make a chart or Venn diagram illustrating the similarities and differences.
6. Why do you think the family feels let down after the Osages have gone by? Describe their feelings and what is behind them.

# *Little House on the Prairie* *(cont.)*

## Chapter Discussions and Activities *(cont.)*

### Chapter 25: Soldiers

1. Plant a variety of vegetable seeds to watch them grow.

2. Do you think Pa's decision to leave is the right one?  Should he make this decision on his own?

3. What does Pa mean when he says "There's no great loss without some small gain"?

### Chapter 26: Going Out

1. Laura enjoys traveling in a covered wagon because of the sense of adventure and opportunity.  How do you think you would like it?

## Culminations

1. Throughout the book, Laura tells of family rules, such as "Do not sing at the table."  Make a chart showing in one column the Ingalls family rules that are given in the book and, in another column, your family rules.

2. As a class, do several household chores as the Ingalls family did them.  Compare these methods with the way in which they are done today.  Calculate the time difference between the Ingalls way and the modern way.

3. It is clear in this novel that nearly everything the Ingalls family needs they hunt, find, or make for themselves.  List and describe the things you and your family do for yourselves.  Then, list and describe those things for which the Ingalls family manages on its own but for which you are dependent on others.  Finally, answer this question: Do you think you and your family could survive a year under the conditions in which the Ingalls family lives throughout this book?

4. In several places through the book, Laura transcribes the sounds animals make.  She often does not use the traditional sounds, such as *buzz* or *moo,* but more inventive ones that seem, to her, to reflect the actual sounds made by the creatures.  Make a list of these sounds from the book.  Then, write your own sounds for 12 more animals.  These should be original and creative, like the ones that Laura writes.

# In My Family's Wagon

On our journey, my family and I would pack . . . .

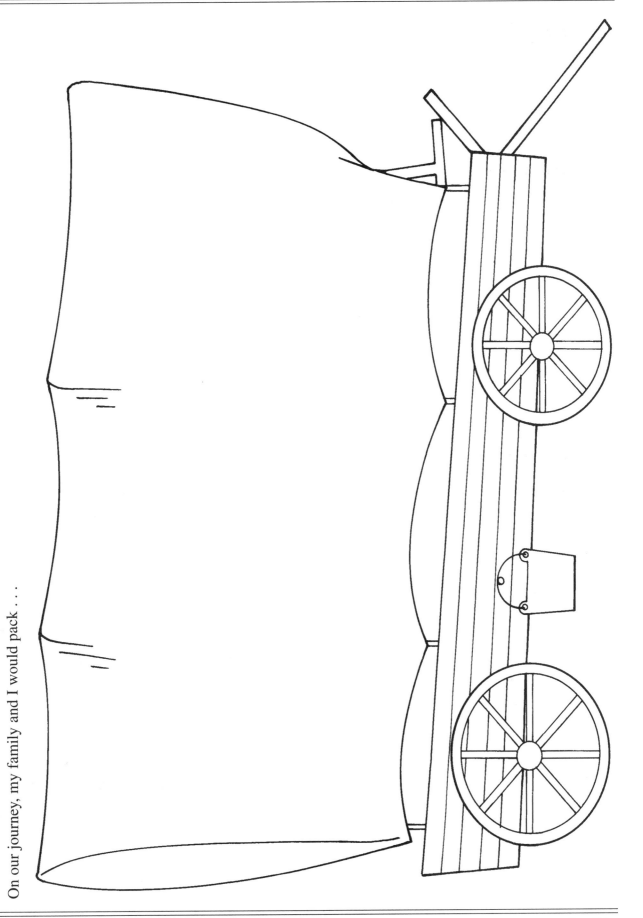

# Across the Tracks

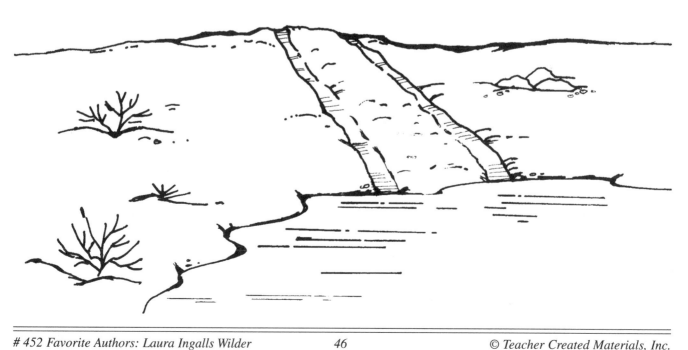

# Building a Log House

You can build a model log house in many ways. Here are two.

## Pretzel House

### Materials:

- long pretzel sticks
- glue
- scissors
- cardboard or wood base
- heavy brown paper
- ruler
- craft knife (Use carefully with adult supervision.)

### Directions:

1. Cut several pretzel sticks in half. Leave the rest whole.*
2. Use two half sticks and two whole sticks to glue in the shape of a rectangle on the cardboard or wood base.
3. Glue additional sticks on top of each of these, constructing the walls of the house. Leave openings for windows and a door.
4. When the walls are as high as you would like them to be, glue two short sticks at a point on each end of the house, making a triangle (the gable end) on top of each short wall. You will first need to cut one end of each so that the sticks can be glued together.
5. Cut paper triangles the size of the gable ends of the house. Glue these over the gable ends to make the walls under the roof.
6. Cut paper strips a little longer than the long sides of the house. They should be about 1" (2.5 cm) wide. Lay these across the top of the house, gluing them to the triangles. Start with the bottom ones first and then overlap them as you move to the top of the roof. Lay the last one over the top, folding it to go over each side. (See chapter 10 which describes Pa's construction of a roof.)
7. Your house is complete. You may add a chimney and scenery if you like.

**\*Challenge:** Carve out notches in each log, laying them into one another just as Pa does. This will give you corners like an actual log house.

## Paper House

### Materials:

- glue
- scissors
- ruler
- cardboard or wood base
- brown paper
- clear tape (optional)

### Directions:

1. Roll strips of brown paper to make logs. Glue or tape them closed.

2. Follow the directions above, using these rolled paper logs instead of pretzels.

# Furnishing the Little House

Color, cut, fold, and glue these furnishings as shown. Place them inside a cardboard box, replicating the interior of the Ingalls family cabin. (Paint wooden spools for the tree stump chairs. Paint a fireplace and windows against the walls. Make a tiny clay shepherdess to place on the mantel.)

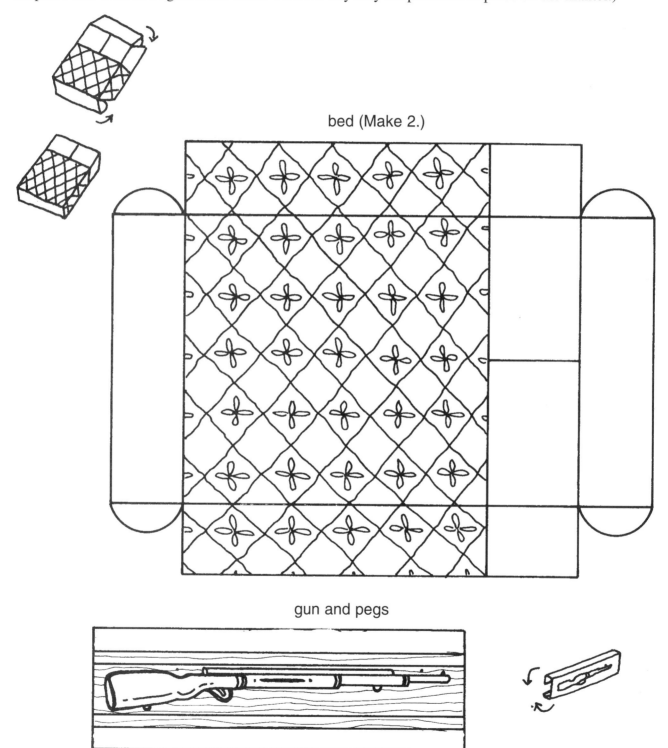

bed (Make 2.)

gun and pegs

# Furnishing the Little House (cont.)

table

mantel

# Furnishing the Little House *(cont.)*

door

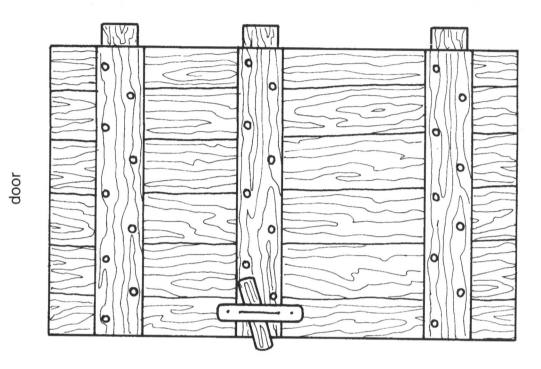

quilt (Use this for the doorway or use the actual door.)

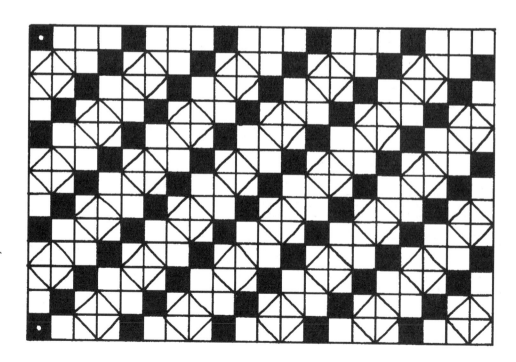

50

# Cat's Cradle

## Materials:

- two yards/meters string, tied in a loop
- your two hands

## Directions:

1. Hang the string on your hands as shown. Stretch your hands apart to make the string loop tight.

2. Pick up the string with your little fingers. The string now crossing the palm of your hands is the palmar string.

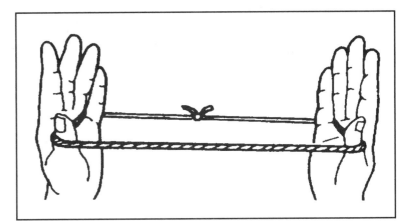

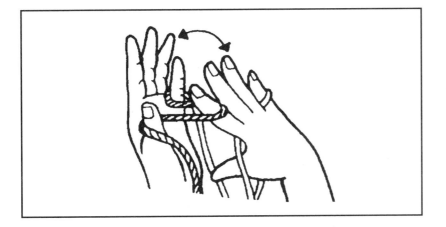

3. Pick up the palmar string of your left hand with the index finger of your right hand. Tighten the string.

4. Pick up the palmar string of your right hand with the index finger of your left hand and tighten the string as shown. This is Cat's Cradle. Do you know any other formations to do?

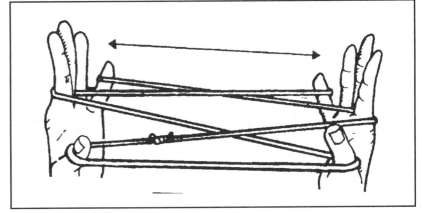

# On the Banks of Plum Creek

*On the Banks of Plum Creek* continues the story of the Ingalls family after they move from the prairies of Kansas. They arrive in Walnut Grove, Minnesota, and begin a new life in a tiny, creekside dugout home. Eventually, they build a new house and grow a promising crop of wheat. The entire family becomes part of the town, and Laura and Mary begin school. (In reality, they both began in Wisconsin when Laura was only four.) They have many joyful experiences together, but hope fades as plagues of grasshoppers beset them and their neighbors, destroying crops and placing the Ingallses in debt. Pa must leave them to find work. In typical fashion, the family rallies, doing what must be done to survive, rediscovering the blessing they always have—one another.

Below and on the pages that follow, you will find individual chapter topics and activities. See page 14 for further explanation.

## Chapter Discussions and Activities

### Chapter 1: The Door in the Ground

1. Find Norway on a map. Research the country, particularly what it was like in the 1870s.
2. Do you think the trades Pa and Mr. Hanson make are fair? Why? Why not?

### Chapter 2: The House in the Ground

1. Locate photographs or actual plantings of morning glories.
2. With clay and straw, make a model of the dugout house.
3. Why do you think Laura would rather sleep outdoors than be safe in the house under the ground?

### Chapter 3: Rushes and Flags

1. Around her new home, Laura notices the flowers blooming, birds singing, and creek rolling. Sit outside your home for a few minutes. What do you notice? (See page 57.)
2. Make things of drinking straws just as Laura and Mary make things of rushes.

### Chapter 4: Deep Water

1. If you went to the swimming hole, would you play it safe like Mary or be like Laura?
2. Do you think Laura will obey Pa about the water from now on?

### Chapter 5: Strange Animal

1. Have you ever followed a temptation, even though you were not supposed to? What happened?
2. Laura has a guilty conscience about going to the swimming hole and decides to tell Pa. What would you have done in her situation? How would you feel about a punishment such as Laura's?
3. Research badgers to find how and why they make themselves flat.

### Chapter 6: Wreath of Roses

1. Brainstorm a list of things you can play on the big gray rock.
2. An a magazine or picture book, try to find a picture of someone who looks like Johnny Johnson.
3. As the Ingalls family moves, they find different communities have people of various cultural backgrounds. Use atlases and other resources to find at least 10 communities within the United States or Canada with strong ties to one cultural group in particular.

# *On the Banks of Plum Creek* (cont.)

## Chapter Discussions and Activities *(cont.)*

**Chapter 7: Ox on the Roof**

1. Laura and Mary have chores to do each day. What daily chores do you have?

2. Imagine you are Laura and you need to bring in the cattle. What would you do in her situation?

**Chapter 8: Straw-Stack**

1. What is a *scythe* and what does it do? Draw a picture of one.

2. Do Laura and Mary disobey Pa when they roll down the stack? What is Pa's reaction to their rolling instead of sliding?

**Chapter 9: Grasshopper Weather**

1. Research plums. Dry plums in the sun. Do they taste different from fresh ones?

2. Research hornets—how they look and live. What do you think "grasshopper weather" is?

**Chapter 10: Cattle in the Hay**

1. What is *challis*? What is an *ox goad*?

2. Mary and Laura are nine and seven when their parents leave them home alone for a day. Would that be possible or practical today? Compare their situation with modern times.

3. What would you have done if faced with cattle in the hay just as Mary and Laura are?

**Chapter 11: Runaway**

1. Have you ever been in a near-miss auto accident such as Pa and Ma nearly experience in their wagon? What did it feel like?

2. Why do you think Laura likes wolves better than cattle?

**Chapter 12: The Christmas Horses**

1. Make mashed potatoes, one of the foods the Ingallses eat at Thanksgiving. (See page 58.)

2. Learn about the first Thanksgiving and how it has been celebrated throughout the years.

3. Eat parched corn. You can buy some in the supermarket or make some of your own. A recipe can be found in *The Little House Cookbook* by Barbara M. Walker (Harper Trophy, 1979).

4. Ma has a wonderful way of explaining Santa Claus to Laura and Mary. If you were a parent, what would you tell your child about Santa if he or she asked?

5. What would each member of your family want for a special gift if you could get anything?

**Chapter 13: Merry Christmas**

1. Collect unused buttons from wherever possible. Make a button string, or, as a class, make a record-length button string. Make it as beautiful as you can, just as Laura and Mary do.

2. Gather and sort buttons. How many ways can you categorize them?

3. Ma has a huge assortment of buttons in many designs. Use your imagination to create a variety of buttons. (See page 59.)

4. Brainstorm for a list of rainy-day things you can do indoors.

5. If possible, ride a horse. How does it feel?

# On the Banks of Plum Creek (cont.)

## Chapter Discussions and Activities (cont.)

### Chapter 14: Spring Freshet

1. Describe the fiercest (or mildest) rain you have ever experienced.

### Chapter 15: The Footbridge

1. Brainstorm the qualities and uses of water. Tell of an experience with a power such as water.

### Chapter 16: The Wonderful House

1. Plant a spring garden.
2. If possible, watch a house being built. Make things from wood shavings and sawdust.
3. What does *a lick and a promise* mean? What does *PAT. 1770* mean?
4. Draw interior pictures of the new house Laura describes, showing every area.

### Chapter 17: Moving In

1. Make curtains like Ma makes. Follow the directions on page 60.
2. Describe the favorite home in which you have lived.

### Chapter 18: The Old Crab and the Bloodsuckers

1. Look up *minnows, crabs,* and *leeches.* Find pictures. Learn how they live and what they do.

### Chapter 19: The Fish-Trap

1. In your own words, describe how the fish trap looks and works.

### Chapter 20: School

1. Have you ever been the "new kid" in school? Do you remember when you first learned to read?

### Chapter 21: Nellie Oleson

1. Mary and Laura share quite a bit, including the books they study and their money. With whom do you share the most? How does it work out?
2. Have you ever known anyone like Nellie Oleson? What do you think makes such people so mean?
3. Have a classroom spell-down (spelling bee). Play ring-around-a-rosy and Uncle John.

### Chapter 22: Town Party

1. What is a *company voice*? What is a *velocipede*?
2. Make models of the various rooms of the Oleson house and store.
3. If anyone has a jumping jack such as the one in the book, bring it in to share. If not, make the jumping jack on pages 61 and 62.
4. Read some Mother Goose rhymes. As a class, choose favorites and illustrate a book of them. Give the book to a primary class.

### Chapter 23: Country Party

1. If you had a party at your home, what games might you and your guests play, using only what you already have around your home?
2. What is vanity? Why are the cakes like vanity?

### Chapter 24: Going to Church

1. If your family attends church, what are the preparations like in your house?
2. How do you think Laura feels about Mrs. Tower?
3. Why do you think Pa gives his three dollars to Rev. Alden instead of buying boots?

# On the Banks of Plum Creek *(cont.)*

## Chapter Discussions and Activities *(cont.)*

**Chapter 25: The Glittering Cloud**

1. Research grasshoppers—how they look and behave. Make a chart of a grasshopper and its body parts.

**Chapter 26: Grasshopper Eggs**

1. Make equations counting the grasshopper eggs, using the basic figures Pa provides.
2. How would you describe Pa after this chapter?

**Chapter 27: Rain**

1. Laura says Mr. Nelson's house looks as if it speaks Norwegian. Find pictures of houses you think might "speak" other languages, such as Spanish, Swahili, etc. Put them together in a class collage.
2. What does the rain after the grasshoppers suggest about nature?

**Chapter 28: The Letter**

1. What is the best letter you ever received? Write a letter to someone special you do not often see.

**Chapter 29: The Darkest Hour Is Just Before Dawn**

1. Was Ma right to give Anna Laura's doll? Was Laura right to take Charlotte back?
2. Tell about a time when you saw someone you loved after many weeks or months.
3. Design a ragdoll face.

**Chapter 30: Going to Town**

1. Listen to recordings of fiddle music. Sing oldtime songs such as the ones Pa plays.

**Chapter 31: Surprise**

1. How does Laura feel toward Nellie? What is the "hot feeling"?
2. As a class, make a Christmas tree like the one in the book. Hang donated presents on the tree. Give the tree to a local charity or family in need.

**Chapter 32: Grasshoppers Walking**

1. Brainstorm for and discuss reasons why the grasshoppers come and why they leave.

**Chapter 33: Wheels of Fire**

1. Ma says that neighbors are some of the best things in life. Make a class list of all the good things in life you can think of. Tell about a special neighbor you have had.

**Chapter 34: Marks on the Slate**

1. Make marks on a paper to represent the days between now and a day you are looking forward to. Each night before bed, mark off one day. Do the marks make the time seem to go faster or slower?

**Chapter 35: Keeping House**

1. Roll sheets of newspapers into logs. Have a class contest to see who can move the most "logs" the quickest. Divide into teams and pile all the newspaper logs at one end of the classroom. At "start," the first person of each team should grab one log and run to the other end of the class, making a team "woodpile." They run back to their teams, touching the hand of the next team members who then each grab a log and run to their woodpiles. When every log has been moved, see which team has the most.

# On the Banks of Plum Creek (cont.)

## Chapter Discussions and Activities (cont.)

### Chapter 36: Prairie Winter

1. Pa must maneuver through the storm, unable to see. Test your skill at doing so. Find a large room or outdoor area that has a few markers in it. One at a time, wear a blindfold, trying to get from one point to another without sight.

2. Laura and Mary know a great many church hymns. How many can your class name?

### Chapter 37: The Long Blizzard

1. Ma's intuition tells her that Pa should not take the trip to town, but Pa does not listen. Have you ever had a feeling or intuition that you did not listen to and should have? What happened? Have you ever followed your intuition and learned that you were right?

### Chapter 38: The Day of Games

1. Play pussy-in-the-corner at home with your family on a stormy day.

2. Create a picture story like the one Ma tells.

3. Find the story of "The House That Jack Built."

4. If you have frosty windows, make thimble pictures as Laura and Carrie do. If not, with a pencil trace circles around the thimbles onto paper in order to make your thimble pictures.

### Chapter 39: The Third Day

1. The whole prairie world is covered with snow. Make snow pictures by using black construction paper and white chalk. Use the chalk to make the snow as it covers the house, trees, and fields. Do not draw in the other objects in the picture. You should be able to tell the shapes of things the snow covers by the way the snow is drawn.

### Chapter 40: The Fourth Day

1. Using clay and other materials, construct a model of what Pa's snow cave must have looked like.

2. Imagine staying three days in a small, dark place, unable to move much and with very little food. What would you do to occupy the time while you were not sleeping?

### Chapter 41: Christmas Eve

1. Make up songs for your everyday activities like the one Pa sings for Laura and Mary to set and clear the table.

2. Make cornbread like the type the Ingalls family eats on Christmas Eve. (See page 63.)

## Culminations

1. Learn about quilting, especially nine-patch and the bear-claw pattern Laura makes. Make quilt blocks. If desired, put them together as a class quilt. Raffle off the quilt as a fundraiser or donate it to charity.

2. Oxen and cattle play an important part in this book. Learn about cattle—caring for them, herding them, milking them, and so on. Prepare a class report, complete with charts and visual aids.

3. Research schools of the late 1800s. Construct a model schoolhouse and outline a typical day. For a day or a week, conduct school in the same manner as was done in that time period.

4. Learn about Christmas celebrations of the late 1800s. Prepare a Christmas party in that style.

# Around My Home

Here is what I sense around my home.

| Sights | Sounds | Smells | Textures | Tastes |
|--------|--------|--------|----------|--------|
|        |        |        |          |        |

# Mashed Potatoes

The Ingalls family enjoys mashed potatoes as part of their Thanksgiving feast. Follow this recipe to make some of your own.

## Ingredients:

- one dozen potatoes
- water to cover the potatoes
- five tbsp. (75 mL) butter
- one cup (250 mL) milk
- salt to taste
- pepper to taste

## Materials:

- potato peeler or paring knife
- fork
- knife
- large kettle
- potato masher
- large, sturdy spoon
- serving dish

## Preparation:

1. Peel the potatoes and cut them into about eight pieces each.
2. Place the potatoes and water in the kettle. Cook over a medium heat.
3. Check the potatoes after 15 to 20 minutes by piercing one or two with a fork. If the fork goes through easily, they are ready. If not, cook longer until they are very soft.
4. Drain the potatoes. Begin to mash them with the potato masher.
5. Add the milk and butter. Continue mashing until the potatoes are completely mashed and the butter is melted.
6. With the spoon, whip the potatoes as quickly and thoroughly as you can. (You may also use an electric beater.)
7. Mix in salt and pepper to taste.
8. Place in the serving dish and enjoy. (If you wish to brown the top of the potatoes, put them in a heatable serving dish and place them in a warm oven for a few minutes until the top is golden brown.)

# Buttons

Design and color these one-dozen buttons.

**Challenge:** How many more designs can you think of?  Draw them on the back or on additional paper.

# Making Curtains

Ma makes white muslin curtains with calico trim. You can make a smaller version. Here is how.

## Materials:

- 12" x 12" (30 cm x 30 cm) white muslin
- 12" x 3" (30 cm x 7.5 cm) calico or patterned fabric
- straight pins
- sewing needle
- thread (white or the primary color of the colored fabric)
- scissors
- iron and ironing board

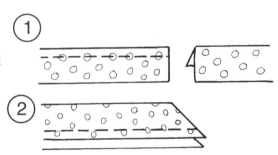

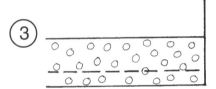

## Directions:

*To attach the trim* (calico or patterned fabric)

1. Fold toward the back ¼" (.6 cm) along the top edge of the calico or patterned fabric. Press along the fold with the iron.

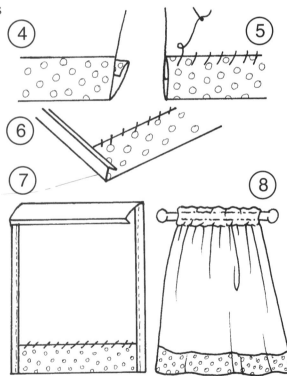

2. Line up the creased edge of the calico with an edge of the muslin so that the right sides (fronts) face each other on the inside and the backs of the fabrics are on the outside. Pin along the crease and use a running stitch (following the pins) to sew the trim onto the calico.

3. Fold ¼" (.6 cm) along the other long edge of the calico trim. Press under with an iron.

4. Fold the trim toward the back of the muslin, lining up the front and back folds of the trim so that the trim is equal on both sides of the muslin.

5. Press down the trim once again so that it is smooth and lies flat on both sides. To complete the trim, pin and sew (using a hem stitch) the back folded edge of the trim to the muslin.

*To hem the curtain sides*

6. To hem one side of the curtain, fold and press the side edge under (toward the back) ¼" (.6 cm). Repeat for a second fold. Pin the folds in place. Follow the same procedure for the other curtain side.

7. Stitch to finish the side hems.

*To make the top pocket* (for the rod)

8. Follow steps 6 and 7, but make the second fold 1" (2.5 cm) or more to allow for the size of the rod.

# Jumping Jack

You can make your own jumping jack doll, a paper version similar to the wood one Nellie Oleson has. Follow these directions.

## Materials:

- patterns (page 62)
- thin cardboard
- scissors
- crayons or marking pens
- one large bead
- yarn or string
- large nail
- pencil
- brass paper fasteners

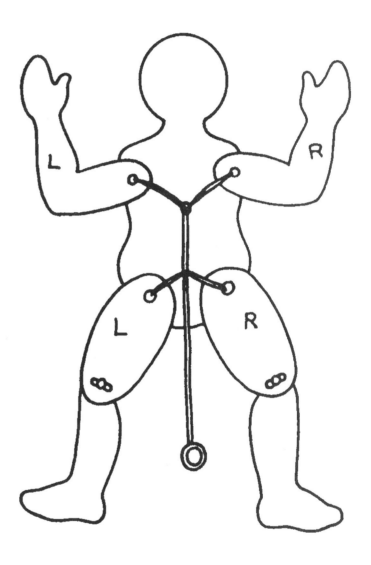

## Directions:

1. Trace the pattern pieces onto the cardboard.

2. Color the pieces with crayons or marking pens.

3. Cut out the pieces, keeping track so that you know which piece is which body part.

4. Attach each body section at the X's with the fasteners opened in the back.

5. String the jumping jack together as shown. Knot the string at the dots on the arms and thighs.

6. Tie the large bead to the end of the string.

7. Hold the jumping jack on his body or head. Pull the string. His arms and legs will move up and down.

# Jumping Jack *(cont.)*

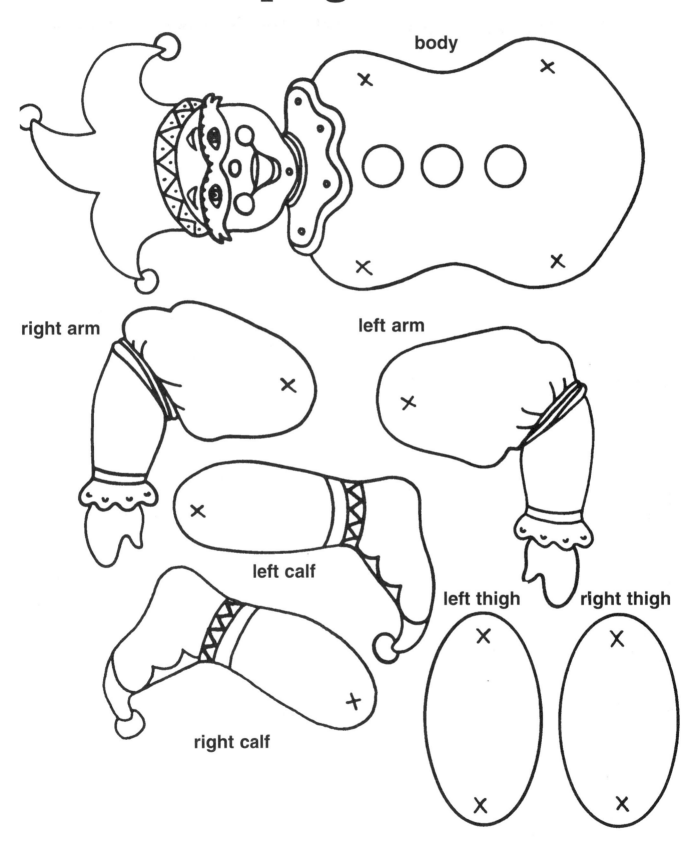

body

right arm

left arm

left calf

left thigh   right thigh

right calf

# Corn Bread

The corn bread Ma made was probably made entirely from cornmeal, water, and salt. This corn bread recipe is a little richer. It yields about nine servings.

## Ingredients:

- 1 cup (250 mL) yellow cornmeal
- 1 cup (250 mL) all-purpose flour
- 2 tablespoons (30 mL) sugar
- 4 teaspoons (40 mL) baking powder
- ½ (2.5 mL) teaspoon salt
- 1 cup (250 mL) milk
- ¼ cup (63 mL) shortening
- 1 egg

## Directions:

1. Heat the oven to 425° F (220° C).
2. Blend all ingredients and then beat vigorously by hand for about 1 minute.
3. Pour the mixture into a greased pan (8" x 8" x 2" / 20 cm x 20 cm x 5 cm).
4. Bake until golden brown about 20–25 minutes.

# By the Shores of Silver Lake

*By the Shores of Silver Lake* follows *On the Banks of Plum Creek* in the Little House series but skips the next series of events in the lives of the Ingalls family. Missing are their lives in a rented home in Walnut Grove, their year in Burr Oak, Iowa, running the Masters Hotel, the birth and death of their son Charles Frederick, and an attempt by a rich neighbor to adopt Laura. After this, the family moved back to Walnut Grove where Pa worked as a carpenter, butcher, and miller, among other things. In the spring of 1879, scarlet fever struck the family, and it is after this that the story continues in *By the Shores of Silver Lake*.

In this fifth novel of the series originally intended as one long novel, the family has an opportunity to move from Walnut Grove, Minnesota, where their lives are stagnating, westward to the Dakota Territory. Their dreams are renewed as they follow the railroad camp and establish their home as the first settlers in the new town of De Smet. This was to be the final big move for Pa and Ma Ingalls. It is here that they lived out the rest of their lives and finally found a measure of prosperity. It is also here that Laura meets and marries the "farmer boy" of her second novel, Almanzo Wilder.

Below and on the pages that follow, you will find individual chapter topics and activities. See page 14 for further explanation.

## Chapter Discussions and Activities

### Chapter 1: Unexpected Visitor

1. Research scarlet fever, its past treatment, and how it is treated today.
2. Pa sells his small farm for two hundred dollars. Can you determine what such a farm might sell for at today's prices?
3. Have you ever traveled by train? Tell about your experience.

### Chapter 2: Grown Up

1. Have you ever had a pet die? Tell about it and how you felt.
2. Laura writes that being grown up means that you take care of yourself. What do you think makes a person grown up? (See page 70.)

### Chapter 3: Riding in the Cars

1. How does an Ingalls family move compare to a move your family might make? Make a chart with two columns to show the differences or a Venn diagram to show the differences and similarities.
2. What is *delaine*?
3. Watch a train move. How would you describe it?
4. Why do you think trains are so frightening and exciting to Laura?
5. Feel some velvet. How would you describe it?
6. Research the various jobs on a railroad over time, such as the the jobs of brakeman and conductor mentioned here.
7. Laura describes some people on the train for Mary, speculating about where they are going, what they do, and who they are. Find pictures of people in magazines. For each, write a character sketch based on the clues in the picture. To write an extended character sketch, using your imagination more fully, see the form on page 71.
8. Use a shoebox to make a model of the inside of a train car as described by Laura.

# *By the Shores of Silver Lake* (cont.)

## Chapter Discussions and Activities (cont.)

**Chapter 4: End of the Rails**

1. Draw a picture of a railroad turntable or find one in a book.

2. Laura wishes that Pa was a railroad man. What do you wish your parents did?

3. Describe how you think each of the family feels while eating and waiting at the hotel in Tracy.

**Chapter 5: Railroad Camp**

1. Laura says a day of little jolts is tiring. What does she mean?

2. If you had to ride in a wagon all day, what might you do to keep yourself occupied?

3. Discuss why Hi and Docia might be in debt after working all summer for the company.

**Chapter 6: The Black Ponies**

1. What do you think of Lizzie's marriage? How is Laura like the black ponies?

2. What does "like butter wouldn't melt in your mouths" mean? What is the difference between *trot* and *gallop*?

**Chapter 7: The West Begins**

1. What is a *surveyor*? What does a surveyor do?

2. Laura writes, ". . . there are so many ways of seeing things . . . ." What does she mean?

3. Each member of the Ingalls family has a perspective on the current move and journey across the Dakota prairie. In your own words, describe how Pa, Ma, and Laura each feels about it.

**Chapter 8: Silver Lake**

1. What is a *slough*? Research wild ducks, geese, herons, cranes, and pelicans.

2. Walking to the lake, Carrie and Mary want to turn back, but Laura wishes she could go on with the wild birds. Who do you think you would be most like in this situation?

3. Mary learns about her environment just by listening. Close your eyes and listen for as long as you can. What do you hear? Can you tell what is happening around you?

**Chapter 9: Horse Thieves**

1. Do you think Big Jerry is a horse thief? What do you think Pa does when he leaves at night?

**Chapter 10: The Wonderful Afternoon**

1. What do you think of Ma's definition of a lady?

2. Laura, Lena, and Pa know songs for every occasion. Write a song to describe what Laura sees during her "wonderful afternoon."

3. In your own words, describe the railroad work Laura watches.

4. Pa says that Laura will live to see a time when nearly everyone travels by railroad. Does she? List steps to build a railroad. Make a picture chart showing transportation through the ages.

5. How is the railroad work like music? Find a piece of music that you think sounds like the railroad work might sound.

6. Do you think what Pa says is true, that "If enough people think of a thing and work hard enough at it, . . . it's pretty nearly bound to happen"?

## Chapter Discussions and Activities *(cont.)*

### Chapter 11: Payday

1. Complete some time-check math equations. (See page 72.)
2. What does Ma mean by "better a live dog than a dead lion"?
3. After this chapter, how would you describe Laura?

### Chapter 12: Wings Over Silver Lake

1. The Ingallses are sorrowful to have killed a swan, but they do not seem to feel such remorse over the pelican. They will not eat either one. Why the difference in feeling? Discuss responses.
2. How do you feel about Pa and Ma telling Laura to teach school? Laura writes that all she could do at that time to earn money was to teach school. How have times changed for women since then?

### Chapter 13: Breaking Camp

1. In this chapter are two stories of people trying to bring about their own justice—Uncle Hi with the railroad and Mr. Boast with Pete. Are the actions of each justified? What do you think?

### Chapter 14: The Surveyors' House

1. The surveyors' house is like a palace to Laura. It is larger and better supplied than any home in which she has lived. Describe what would be your own palace-type home.
2. In your own words, write the meaning of the canoe song.

### Chapter 15: The Last Man Out

1. What is *consumption*? Why was the prairie thought to cure it?
2. Listen to some polka music. Learn to dance the polka. In this chapter, Laura and Mary learn to dance the polka. How many other dances can the class name? How many can you dance?
3. What is one of the nicest winter evenings you have spent with your family? What did you do?

### Chapter 16: Winter Days

1. Learn to play checkers. (See page 73.) Have a classroom checkers challenge.

### Chapter 17: Wolves on Silver Lake

1. Draw a picture of Silver Lake in moonlight. Let your imagination tell what lies at the end of the moonpath.
2. When Laura tells Pa that they followed the moonpath, he says, "You would!" What does Pa mean?
3. Why do you think Laura does not want Pa to catch the wolf?

### Chapter 18: Pa Finds the Homestead

1. Why do you think the wolves did not chase Laura and Carrie? What role do they have in Pa finding the homestead?

### Chapter 19: Christmas Eve

1. On Christmas Eve, the family reminisces about their Christmases of the past. Think of a special yearly event in your own home or school. Which was your favorite? What made it so special?

### Chapter 20: The Night Before Christmas

1. Define and find recordings of the voices listed in the book: bass, tenor, soprano, alto, contralto, and treble.
2. Have you ever had a surprise visit at home? Did you like it? Was it hard to make room for visitors? Was it worth the effort?

# By the Shores of Silver Lake *(cont.)*

## Chapter Discussions and Activities *(cont.)*

### Chapter 21: Merry Christmas

1. If you were to make presents for everyone in your family from things you have around your home, what could you make?

2. In this chapter, Pa speaks of "solid comfort." What does he mean? What is solid comfort for you?

3. At home one evening, enjoy popcorn and checkers with your family instead of doing the usual things. How do you like it?

### Chapter 22: Happy Winter Days

1. Divide into small groups. One group at a time will write a section of a story. Leave the story at a climactic part, and then pass the story on to the next group. Go around one or more times to each group. When finished, give each student a copy of the complete "continued story" to share with their families and friends at home.

2. If you had no contact with the outside world, including no newspapers, radio, or television, imagine how important books and stories would be to you. Think about this. Then, consider living in an isolated area and imagine that you could take only 10 pieces of reading material with you. Which 10 would you choose?

3. Construct a *whatnot* from cardboard according to the directions given in this chapter.

4. As a class, sing "Three Blind Mice" in a round as long as you can.

### Chapter 23: On the Pilgrim Way

1. In this chapter, the Ingalls family learns of a college for the blind. What they do not know is that a method called Braille has been developed so the blind can read and write. Louis Braille designed the Braille alphabet and system of writing. Page 74 shows how the alphabet appears. You may wish to locate a copy of the alphabet or a book that shows actual Braille with raised dots so that the students can close their eyes and attempt to distinguish the letters through touch. If possible, have small groups or individuals devise ways to make the raised dots of Braille.

2. Prepare a class recipe (receipt) book. Include in it a favorite recipe from each student's family. Call it *Brother Stuart's Recipes for Baching*.

3. Research to find information about De Smet, the Jesuit missionary priest from Belgium.

4. Missionaries were important, influential figures in the expanding West. Research more about their work during the 1800s.

### Chapter 24: The Spring Rush

1. What is a *greenhorn*?

2. What does Ma mean by "Might as well be hung for a sheep as a lamb"?

3. Why are so many people traveling west? Do some research if you need to.

### Chapter 25: Pa's Bet

1. In Pa's situation, what would you have done?

2. Why does Pa believe that "everything is more or less a gamble"?

3. Is Pa's bet a good one—14 dollars against 160 acres and five years?

# By the Shores of Silver Lake *(cont.)*

## Chapter Discussions and Activities *(cont.)*

### Chapter 26: The Building Boom

1. Would you be willing to do the work the Ingalls family does to make money?
2. What is *sage*?
3. Find recipes for sage dressing and for onion dressing. If possible, make them both and compare. Make a class graph showing who chooses which.
4. Due to the building boom, hunting will be scarce. Make a list of all the new town's pros and cons for the Ingalls family.

### Chapter 27: Living in Town

1. Why does the town make Laura feel "lonely and scared" on the prairie?
2. Discuss what Pa means when he tells what it takes to build up a country.
3. Often in this book, Laura compares herself to a wild bird. What is the comparison?
4. Learn about *claim jumping*—what it is and how it happened.

### Chapter 28: Moving Day

1. How do you feel about moving?
2. How are the brown horses with black tails and manes like Laura?
3. Sketch the unfinished claim shanty as Laura describes it.

### Chapter 29: The Shanty on the Claim

1. Draw a map showing how Ma and Laura fit all the furniture in the little claim shanty. (See page 75.)
2. Find a sample of tar paper to see and to feel.
3. What reasons might the government have had for creating tree claims?
4. Find out about cottonwood trees. Find one growing in your area. Study its composition and its leaves.
5. Souvenir twigs from the cottonwoods that Pa planted can be obtained from the Laura Ingalls Wilder Memorial Society in De Smet. For an address, see page 108.

### Chapter 30: Where Violets Grow

1. Study and find violets. Grow some.
2. Learn about buffalo wallows and why the buffalo made them.
3. Laura imagines fairies in a fairy ring, and Ma admonishes her for foolish thought. What does this suggest about each of their characters? What do you think Pa thinks of fairy rings? How about Mary?
4. According to myth, horseshoes are said to bring luck. How many other things can you name that are supposed to be lucky?
5. Pa decides to raise cattle instead of farming. What reasons might he have for this decision?

# By the Shores of Silver Lake *(cont.)*

## Chapter Discussions and Activities *(cont.)*

### Chapter 31: Mosquitoes

1. Research to find why Pa prefers the cattle out in the summer.
2. Why does a smudge stop the mosquitoes?
3. What is *mosquito bar*?

### Chapter 32: Evening Shadows Fall

1. There are many songs and poems about Barbara Allen. How many can the class find?
2. The final chapter paints a picture of the feeling in the new home. What is the picture? What does the picture say?

## Culminations

1. Research the railroad system of the late 1800s and the effect it had on westward advancement in the United States. If possible, take a class field trip to a railroad station and, even better, take a train ride. Be aware of museums and exhibits that show old trains and train paraphernalia.

2. Laura is asked to be Mary's eyes. Choose various sights for each student to describe "for Mary." Share the descriptions while the students close their eyes. Discuss how well the writings paint the pictures.

   You might also have each student select a sight and then describe it as clearly as possible, painting a picture with words. Back in class, each can read his or her writing, and the others can try to imagine the sights. Ask the class to name some of the clearest descriptions and discuss what makes them so. This will be a wonderful opportunity to enhance their writing skills.

   Over time, ask the students to be aware of such descriptions in the books they read and to share any particularly good ones with the class. Collect them all in a book entitled *Eyes for Mary.*

3. Make a songbook of all the songs listed in this book. Research the melodies of each. Learn the songs and host a Little House concert, adding other songs from the time if you like.

4. Since so much of their lives were spent in dealing with day-to-day survival, Laura writes vividly of the food they enjoyed. Make a list of all the food mentioned in this book. Prepare several authentic recipes together and enjoy them in a class party.

5. Research homesteading, how it developed, what it involved, and the people and land it affected. For a challenge, construct a model homesteader's shanty out of large cardboard boxes and other materials. (See pages 104–107.)

6. This book is filled with the beliefs and philosophies of Ma and Pa Ingalls. Write an essay explaining them, including the many maxims they use and examples of how their actions support their beliefs. In conclusion, add how and what each girl (except Grace), particularly including Laura, has learned from her parents. Give examples to support what you write.

7. More than anything, Laura is struck by the big sky of the Dakota prairie. Paint a class mural of a big sky and hang it in your classroom. On it, write words and phrases that show how one feels under such a big sky. If possible, take a trip to locations where one can feel such openness.

# Grown Up

Brainstorm for all the ways to complete the following statement.

When I am grown up, I will . . .

_____    _____

_____    _____

_____    _____

_____    _____

_____    _____

_____    _____

_____    _____

Choose one item from your list above and write a paragraph explaining it.

# Character Sketch

Name _____

Nickname _____

Date of Birth _____

Place of Birth _____

Occupation _____

_____

Favorite Things (color, book, movie, food, television show, hobby, season, holiday, etc.)

_____

_____

_____

_____

_____

_____

_____

Dislikes _____

_____

Family Connections _____

_____

_____

_____

# Time-Checks

Each man's time-check shows the *days worked*, *money owed* to the store, and *board bill*. The last two are subtracted from the first.

If a man earns one dollar a day, figure out each of the following problems.

| **Pay = days worked - money owed to store - board bill** |
|:--:|

1. days worked = 20

   money owed = $5.00

   board bill = $4.50

   **pay =** ☐

2. days worked = 30

   money owed = $7.50

   board bill = $6.75

   **pay =** ☐

3. days worked = 45

   money owed = $10.35

   board bill = $10.13

   **pay =** ☐

4. days worked = 25

   money owed = $3.23

   board bill = $5.63

   **pay =** ☐

5. days worked = 22

   money owed = $3.92

   board bill = $4.95

   **pay =** ☐

6. days worked = 35

   money owed = $9.10

   board bill = $7.88

   **pay =** ☐

7. days worked = 15

   money owed = $1.85

   board bill = $3.38

   **pay =** ☐

8. days worked = 27

   money owed = $4.19

   board bill = $6.08

   **pay =** ☐

9. days worked = 50

   money owed = $7.36

   board bill = $11.25

   **pay =** ☐

10. days worked = 58

    money owed = $12.62

    board bill = $13.05

    **pay =** ☐

# Playing Checkers

Make a checkerboard and playing pieces with whatever materials you have available.

To play, follow these directions. Black plays first, moving piece A, B, C, or D along a diagonal to another dark square in the row above. (See diagram.) Red moves next in the same way. After this, the players take turns moving one piece at a time toward the opponent's back row (9, 10, 11, 12 or I, J, K, L). Players can only move to unoccupied black squares.

If an opponent's playing piece is in the next diagonal black square and the square next in the diagonal line is unoccupied, the player must jump the opponent's playing piece and capture it. The captured piece is removed from the board. If there is more than one jump possible in the same diagonal, all jumps must be made. If a playing piece reaches the back row of the opponent's side, that piece now becomes a "king." The opponent places a captured playing piece on top of the king. A king can move in any direction on adjoining black squares. Kings can capture playing pieces just like regular pieces can; however, they can move either forward or backward.

The winner is the first player either to capture all the opponent's pieces or to corner the opponent so that he or she cannot move.

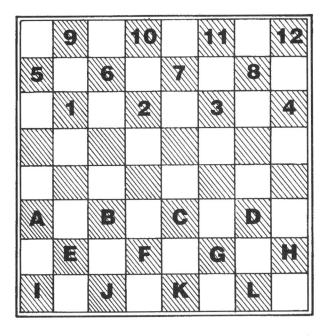

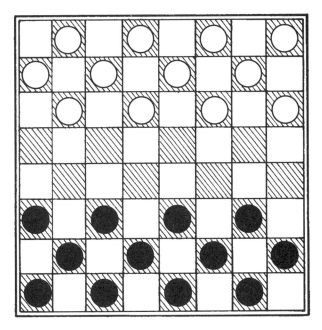

# Braille Alphabet and System of Writing

Louis Braille, born January 4, 1809, was blind from the time he was a young child. He developed a raised-dot-alphabet and writing system for the blind. Originally, individuals could use a special slate and tool to press the dots into heavy paper for blind people to read with their fingertips. Today, special machines can do the same work.

Here is the Braille alphabet and four words with their own dot code. (They are shown as they appear visually. Technically, they would be raised dots on the paper.) Use this system of dots to write your name and a message for a classmate. Trade papers to read one another's messages.

| A | B | C | D | E | F | G | H | I | J |
|---|---|---|---|---|---|---|---|---|---|

| K | L | M | N | O | P | Q | R | S | T |
|---|---|---|---|---|---|---|---|---|---|

| U | V | W | X | Y | Z | and | of | the | with |
|---|---|---|---|---|---|-----|----|-----|------|

**Name:**

**Message:**

# Claim Shanty

Inside this room (aerial view), fit the doorway, two windows, three bedsteads, curtains, two rocking chairs, whatnot, stove, food cupboard, trunk, and table as they are described in the book.

# The Long Winter

The sixth book in the series, *The Long Winter* (working title: *The Hard Winter*) tells of the Ingalls family and De Smet surviving one of the hardest, longest winters recorded—the winter of 1880–1881. Great areas throughout the midwest lay frozen under relentless blizzards throughout a six-month period of time. Homesteaders and citizens of new towns like De Smet lived without support from the outside world, and some did not survive. However, the Ingalls family and the citizens of De Smet did, and they went on to prosper.

No novel in the series shows quite so clearly the diligence and survival instincts of the Ingalls family. They utilize every resource possible in surviving the harsh winter. Nearly frozen and starved, they come through intact, typically looking for and finding their blessings. The novel closes with a celebration of their victory over the winter and their hopes for future times.

This novel also shows the character of Almanzo Wilder in depth. Only briefly mentioned in *By the Shores of Silver Lake*, the one-time farmer boy is one of this novel's heros. He and his friend Cap Garland save the entire town from starvation by an act of bravery that brings 60 bushels of wheat to the hungry people. Almanzo, like Charles Ingalls, is willing to do whatever needs to be done in order to survive and prosper. It is no wonder that one day he and Laura find their way together.

Below and on the pages that follow, you will find individual chapter topics and activities. See page 14 for further explanation.

## Chapter Discussions and Activities

### Chapter 1: Make Hay While the Sun Shines

1. What is a *mowing machine*? How does it work?
2. Why does Pa cover the jug with grass?
3. Research garter snakes. If possible, study a live one.
4. What are the family's objections to Laura working in the fields? What do you think of their ideas?
5. What is a *windrow*? What is a *haycock*? What is a *whiffletree*?
6. Make ginger water. (See page 82.)
7. Research muskrats. Find a diagram of a muskrat home.
8. Pa names one major difference between animals and people. What others can you name?

### Chapter 2: An Errand to Town

1. What is a false front? Find an illustration or photograph of one. Why were they made?
2. In a book entitled *Laura Ingalls Wilder Country* (see bibliography, page 111) you can find a map of De Smet circa 1883. Share it with the class, enlarging it to hang on the wall while you read the story. Point out pertinent areas on the map as you read.
   **Alternative:** Construct a map of the town based on Laura's descriptions. This would be a good small-group project.
3. The replacement part for Pa's mowing machine costs five cents. Do some research to find out what else five cents would buy in 1880. Compare that to what five cents might buy today.
4. Carrie feels safe with Laura. With whom do you feel safe?
5. What does Laura mean when she writes that Carrie is old enough "to be really a sister"?
6. Fabricate tall grasses to demonstrate how Laura and Carrie feel wandering through them, unable to see where they are going.

# *The Long Winter* (cont.)

## Chapter Discussions and Activities (cont.)

**Chapter 3: Fall of the Year**

1. What is the "equinoctial storm"?
2. Grow a vegetable garden. Experience digging in the dirt for potatoes. How does it feel?
3. Try sewing a seam as Laura describes. How easy is it?
4. Make a pumpkin pie. Also, make an apple pie and compare the two. Are the tastes alike?

**Chapter 4: October Blizzard**

1. Make and drink cambric tea.
2. Listen to marches. Keep time to their beats.

**Chapter 5: After the Storm**

1. Why is Laura so horrified at the sight of the cattle?
2. Research auks. What do they look like? How and where do they live?
3. What kind of bird might this bird have been?

**Chapter 6: Indian Summer**

1. What is an *Indian summer*?

**Chapter 7: Indian Warning**

1. There have been many indications so far that the coming winter will be a long, hard one. Name the indications.
2. If you were in Harthorn's store that day in 1880, would you listen to the Indian's warning? What would you do in response?
3. Ma has strong prejudices concerning Indians. Why might this be so? Do you think Pa shares her feelings?

**Chapter 8: Settled in Town**

1. What sort of desk does Laura describe? Have you ever seen one?
2. Make a braided rag rug. (See page 83.)
3. Make a list of all the sounds you imagine can make up the sounds of De Smet in 1880. Next, make a list of all the sounds that might make up a modern town.
4. For Pa, what are the pros and cons of living in a settled town? How about for Ma?

**Chapter 9: Cap Garland**

1. Describe Cap Garland, his appearance and character.
2. Laura makes new school friends in this chapter. Who are your school friends? Describe them. What do you have in common?
3. In Miss Garland's place before Mr. Foster comes, what would you do?
4. Have you ever been in a situation where it seems unbearable to go on, but you must go on? Do you know of anyone who has? What happened?
5. Have you ever been lost? How did you feel?
6. What is the worst storm you can remember? What happened? How did you feel?
7. When Laura and Carrie make it home, they see Pa carrying a rope and lantern, ready to come after them. For what would he need the rope and lantern?

# *The Long Winter* (cont.)

## Chapter Discussions and Activities (cont.)

### Chapter 10: Three Days' Blizzard

1. In this chapter, Almanzo thinks about some legal "loopholes." What is a loophole? Can you name and describe any others?
2. Do you think there is a anything wrong with Almanzo filing a claim at age 19?
3. Do you agree that you cannot "lump men together and measure them by any rule"? Why or why not? Write your ideas and/or discuss this as a class.
4. Make buckwheat pancakes. (See page 84.)

### Chapter 11: Pa Goes to Volga

1. Pa goes to help on the train so that he can move about and be useful. In the same circumstances, would you choose to spend a day at hard labor like Pa?
2. Mr. Edwards, in his way, has been a great benefactor to the Ingalls family. What benefactors do you know in your life or in the world? How might you be a benefactor to others?
3. By giving 20 dollars to Mary, Mr. Edwards is helping her dream of college come true. Who has helped you with a special dream you have had? What happened? Write it as a story.

### Chapter 12: Alone

1. Learn to knit. (See page 85.)
2. Share samples of hand-knit items to develop an appreciation for the skill and patience involved in such a craft. Also, bring in machine-knit articles and research the history and composition of this modern machinery.
3. With his fiddle, Pa plays the melody of the storm. Find other pieces of music that seem to replicate the sounds of nature. Share them with the class.
4. Why does Laura shiver even after she is warm?

### Chapter 13: We'll Weather the Blast

1. Ma states clearly that it is wrong to depend on anyone else. Why is this idea important to her?
2. Have a contest to see who can name the most of something, perhaps nursery rhymes, fairy tales, or television shows.
3. Why does Laura change her mind and want to teach school?
4. What is the coldest temperature you have experienced? The warmest? What were they like?

### Chapter 14: One Bright Day

1. What do you think of the Ingalls family rule not to laugh too much at the table?
2. Have you ever been unable to see someone for awhile whom you normally see regularly? How did it feel to see him or her again? What did you want to do or say?
3. If possible, skate on ice in your shoes or skate on a wood floor in your socks. How does it feel?
4. Try a baked potato with salt and another with butter. Compare the tastes.

### Chapter 15: No Trains

1. Bring in samples of lace to compare the different styles. See if anyone you know knows how to make lace and ask them for a classroom demonstration.
2. Why does Laura offer willingly to make Mary's rug?

78

# The Long Winter *(cont.)*

## Chapter Discussions and Activities *(cont.)*

**Chapter 16: Fair Weather**

1. Try to make a sketch of Pa's sled.
2. Write a letter, filling every empty space just as Ma does.

**Chapter 17: Seed Wheat**

1. Should Almanzo sell his wheat? Why or why not? If not, under what conditions should he?

**Chapter 18: Merry Christmas**

1. What does Pa mean by "Needs must, when the devil drives."
2. What is a *hair-receiver*? What is a *hair switch*?
3. Read stories aloud. For tips and an activity, see page 86.
4. Laura falls asleep, hearing sounds from the past in her imagination. What important sounds are from your past? List all you can think of.

**Chapter 19: Where There's a Will**

1. Follow Laura's directions to twist hay. (Or, experiment with cord or strands of yarn.)
2. What is wrong with "folks" depending on things like kerosene?
3. Is it true that "Where there's a will, there's a way"?
4. Research to find how a mill works.

**Chapter 20: Antelope!**

1. Research antelope, what they look like, their habitats, and their behaviors.
2. Mr. Foster acts before thinking, affecting everyone. What are the results of his foolishness?
3. When out on the prairie, Almanzo feels he is the only life around. Have you ever felt that way?

**Chapter 21: The Hard Winter**

1. Read about butchering and how it is done.
2. Pa says it takes patience and perseverance to survive in the West. Explain how this was true.

**Chapter 22: Cold and Dark**

1. Recite speeches and poems. Hold a class speech competition.
2. Find the complete versions of the speeches and poems listed in this chapter.
3. What do you think of the way Mary is treated in the family? Does she have greater capabilities than she is allowed to exhibit?
4. Imagine being covered in snow like De Smet. How would you feel?
5. What is *saleratus*?
6. Have you ever suddenly been unable to do something you used to do well? Tell about it.

**Chapter 23: The Wheat in the Wall**

1. Ma says it is important for the Ingallses to be grateful for what they have. For what are you grateful?
2. Why does Ma react as she does to Pa's suggestion that he go after the wheat?
3. Should Almanzo sell his wheat?

## Chapter Discussions and Activities *(cont.)*

### Chapter 24: Not Really Hungry

1. With what poem does Laura confuse "Old Tubal Cain"?
2. Try some codfish.
3. Research codfish and where they can be found.

### Chapter 25: Free and Independent

1. How much is a bushel? How much is a peck?
2. What is a *tintype?*
3. Why would Almanzo rather make the trip than sell his wheat?
4. What does going after the wheat suggest about Almanzo's character?

### Chapter 26: Breathing Spell

1. Grace and Pa have a special joke together. Do you have a special joke with one or both of your parents?
2. Some of the bachelors play cards to pass the time during this long winter. How many card games do you know?
3. Have a classroom card tournament.
4. Build card houses in small groups for a competition.

### Chapter 27: For Daily Bread

1. If possible, look or go outside at three o'clock in the morning. How would you describe the world you see?

   (**Note:** In this book, Almanzo and Cap are both 19. In reality, this is not true. Laura turned 14 in 1881 and Almanzo turned 24.)
2. Imagine not seeing another person for four or five months. How would you feel? What would you do to occupy your time?
3. How much does the wheat cost Almanzo and Cap all together?
4. Should they stay the night at Mr. Anderson's place, or is it best that they leave?
5. What sort of men must Cap and Almanzo be to make this trip and persevere through the obstacles?

### Chapter 28: Four Days' Blizzard

1. Mary and Laura have a number of disagreements, each one suggesting something about each of their characters. What do these disagreements suggest?
2. Why does Pa yell at the storm?

### Chapter 29: The Last Mile

1. Why don't Almanzo and Cap charge for their labor?
2. Research to find out what makes Almanzo's feet swell after they are frozen. Why does he rub snow on them?
3. What do you think is a fair price for the wheat?
4. Why does Mr. Loftus change his mind about the price?

# *The Long Winter* *(cont.)*

## Chapter Discussions and Activities *(cont.)*

### Chapter 30: It Can't Beat Us

1. In this chapter, Laura feels a light burning inside her. What is that light? Have you ever felt it? Do you think most people have such a light? What are some seemingly unbearable obstacles and challenges you know of from history that people have overcome?

2. Throughout the latter part of this book, the Ingallses live on coarse, brown bread. Bring a variety of breads into class for sampling. After tasting them, decide which bread you could eat on a regular basis for months without any other food to go with it.

3. For a day, try eating nothing but wheat bread, water, and tea. Do you like it? Do you think your nutritional needs are being met?

4. What is a *chinook*?

### Chapter 31: Waiting for the Train

1. The entire family is excited and anxious while waiting for the train. When have you ever felt that way? Write a story about it.

2. Do you think it was justified for the men to break into the train and to take the food?

### Chapter 32: The Christmas Barrel

1. Imagine a Christmas barrel is coming to you and your family. What would you hope to find in it? Write or draw your ideas on page 87.

2. The Ingalls family decides to celebrate Christmas in May. Choose a holiday that is far removed from the current time of year and plan a celebration for it right now in your classroom. Celebrate it traditionally, even though it is the wrong time of year. How does the unorthodox time add to or change the celebration?

### Chapter 33: Christmas in May

1. Make your own cranberry sauce. To do so, wash three cups (750 mL) fresh cranberries and remove their stems. In a saucepan, stir two cups (500 mL) sugar into two cups (500 mL) water and heat them until they boil. Boil for five minutes. Stir in the cranberries and boil again for five minutes. Remove from the heat, cool, cover, and refrigerate for at least eight hours.

2. What does the song mean to you? Rewrite it in your own words.

## Culminations

1. Find out about the homes that various animals construct. Build models of them in small groups, write brief explanations of them, and host an exhibit for the school.

2. Keep a cast of characters as you read this novel. Add pertinent bits of information next to each character's name. When finished, host a class presentation in which different class members portray the various townsfolk, acting out what they do or their most important scenes.

3. Learn about blizzards, what causes them, and their compositions. Do science experiments involving snow, wind, and temperature. You might also conduct experiments concerning different ways and materials with which to heat.

4. The general stores are an important part of this book. Research stores of the period. What did they carry? What did they charge? What affected their prices? What affected their markets?

# Ginger Water

Ma and Carrie surprise Laura and Pa with ginger water to quench their thirsts. Today, something like Gatorade would be drunk for the same effect. To make small servings of ginger water for a class of about 30, follow these directions.

## Ingredients:

- 1 gallon (4 L) water
- 2 cups (500 mL) cider vinegar
- 1½ (25 mL) tablespoons ginger
- 2½ cups (625 mL) brown sugar

## Materials:

- large jug or pitcher with a tight lid
- stirrer

## Preparation:

1. Mix the vinegar, ginger, and brown sugar until the ginger and sugar are dissolved.

2. Add the water. Stir thoroughly by sealing the container and shaking.

3. Serve and enjoy!

# Braided Rag Rug

The Ingalls family used braided rag rugs both for warmth and decoration. To make a small mat in the same style, follow these directions.

## Materials:

- long fabric scraps in various colors
- needle and thread
- scissors
- fabric glue (optional)

## Directions:

1. Tear the fabric into long strips.
2. Sew the strips together to make three long strands, about 2 yards/meters each.
3. When the three strands are the same length and ready, stitch their ends together on one end and braid them.
4. When braided, stitch the other ends so that the strands stay braided.
5. Round the braid into a tight spiral and, on the bottom, stitch it or glue it (with fabric glue) into place. You now have a braided rag rug.

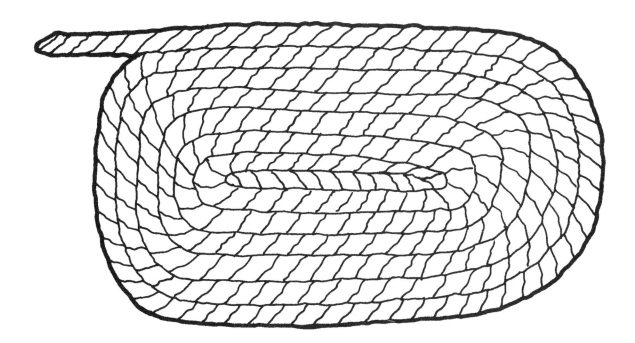

# Buckwheat Pancakes

Make buckwheat pancakes and serve them with molasses, just like Almanzo Wilder does.

## Ingredients:

- 3 eggs
- 3 cups (750 mL) buttermilk
- 6 tablespoons (90 mL) vegetable oil
- 1½ cups (375 mL) flour
- 1½ cups (375 mL) buckwheat flour
- 3 tablespoons (45 mL) sugar
- 3 teaspoons (15 mL) baking powder
- 1½ teaspoons (7.5 mL) soda
- 1½ teaspoons (7.5 mL) salt

## Materials:

- mixing bowl
- stirring spoon
- griddle

## Preparation:

1. Beat the eggs.
2. Add the remaining ingredients and beat them until the batter is smooth.
3. Heat the griddle. Grease it with butter, if desired.
4. Pour the desired amount of batter onto the griddle (about ⅓ cup or 80 mL) per pancake.
5. Flip the pancakes when they bubble and puff.
6. Cook the pancake bottoms until they are golden brown.
7. Serve warm with molasses (or butter and syrup).

# Knitting

Even while sitting, the Ingalls family is never idle. As Laura and Mary sit talking and rocking, they sew and knit. No time is wasted.

You can learn the basics of knitting by following the directions below. With practice, they will become second nature to you, and you can talk or watch television while you knit. Give it a try!

## Materials:

- knitting needles
- yarn

## Directions:

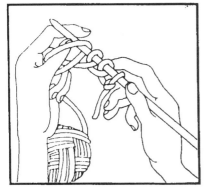

1. Cast on a row of stitches by wrapping them around a knitting needle.

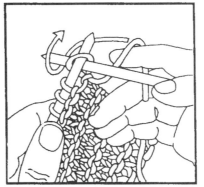

2. Place this needle in your left hand. Insert the tip of your right-hand needle into the top stitch of the left-hand needle.

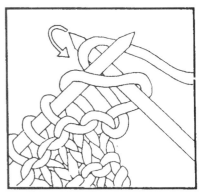

3. Gently pull the yarn forward, keeping it around the tip of the right-hand needle.

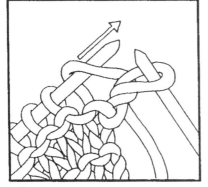

4. Still using the tip of the right-hand needle, pull the yarn through the top stitch.

5. Keeping the new stitch on the right-hand needle, take the top stitch from the left-hand needle.

6. Now you have a complete stitch! Repeat these steps to make more stitches.

# Reading Aloud

A good storyteller will use his or her voice to help tell the story. Scary parts will be told slowly and suspensefully, joyful parts will be told with enthusiasm, and sad parts will be told quietly and tenderly. A good storyteller will also prepare ahead of time, being sure of his story and its purpose so that no stumbling or hemming takes place to lose the listeners' attention. It is also important to . . .

- Read slowly enough to allow listeners to take in everything.

- Read dialogue as the characters would say it. (Dialectal accents are optional.)

- Read only what you enjoy yourself.

- Read what is appropriate for your audience.

- Share the book's pictures with the audience.

Now it is your turn to read aloud. In a small group, select a passage from a novel, storybook, poem, song, speech, or any other reading you enjoy, and prepare to share it aloud. You will prepare the reading as a Readers' Theater, which means that you will "act it out" with your voice only. You will not wear costumes or pantomime actions. Instead, as a group you will use your voices and the words spoken to "show" the audience what is happening. You can read in chorus (together), or group members can have parts and lines. You decide! Practice, practice, practice so that you are all familiar with the reading, and it will flow smoothly when you perform.

As an individual exercise on reading aloud, pick your own reading and then practice alone (with a tape recorder, if possible), read to your family, and even read to your dog if it will listen! Use a lot of expression and be sure to vary your voice level (pitch) so it is not monotonous like Matthew's. Next, back in class, gather into small groups and read your stories to one another. As a member of the audience, practice your listening skills. After each person reads, the group members can tell him or her one thing they really enjoyed about the reading aloud. Comments can be written on pieces of paper and given to the reader if preferred.

---

# Christmas Barrel

What would you like to find in your family's Christmas barrel?  Write or draw everything here.

# Little Town on the Prairie

*Little Town on the Prairie* is the seventh book in the series. It continues the story of the Ingalls family in the year and a half following the long winter. Here, Laura grows to maturity while the town around her also grows. She takes her first job outside the home and continues her education toward earning her teaching certificate. The family begins to prosper in this new town and enjoys the many activities and opportunities the town has to offer. There are socials, literaries, and parties—in short, far more social interaction than is customary for the Ingalls but all very much welcome to them. Best of all, Mary is finally able to attend college. It is for this opportunity that Laura works so hard, and her diligence is rewarded. At age 15, she earns her first teaching certificate and an offer to teach school.

Almanzo Wilder continues to be a character in the series, and in this book he becomes a prospective suitor for Laura. She is somewhat taken aback by his advances, but she is intrigued as well. Although it begins here, their romance does not really blossom until the next book, *These Happy Golden Years*. The beginning of their married life is told in *The First Four Years*. These are the final two books in the series.

Below and on the pages that follow, you will find individual chapter topics and activities. See page 14 for further explanation.

## Chapter Discussions and Activities

### Chapter 1: Surprise

1. What do you imagine the job for Laura can be?
2. At your age, what jobs do you think are available for you? Brainstorm with the class.

### Chapter 2: Springtime on the Claim

1. How do you feel about being outdoors? Can you relate to Laura?
2. Find out about plows and how they are used.
3. If possible, learn to milk a cow.
4. Pa makes a joke about the plow continuing to work on its own. Use your imagination to write a story about another piece of machinery that works on its own.
5. Find out about sheep sorrel.
6. Laura and Mary have a discussion about being good. What do you think about what they say? What do you think about them?

### Chapter 3: The Necessary Cat

1. What is the importance of a county? What are its functions?
2. Learn about cats and kittens. What do tiny kittens need for survival? When do they normally separate from their mothers?

### Chapter 4: The Happy Days

1. These are happy days for the Ingalls family because life is going well and there is promise for the future. What makes the happiest days for you?
2. What is the most amazing animal story you have ever heard?
3. In this chapter, Laura talks with pleasure of the days being nearly the same. In *The Long Winter*, there is frustration and depression over the sameness. What is the difference?

# *Little Town on the Prairie* *(cont.)*

## Chapter Discussions and Activities *(cont.)*

### Chapter 5: Working in Town

1. Research sewing machines. Learn how they were invented. If possible, learn to use one.
2. Compare the amount of time it takes to hand-stitch and machine-stitch seams of a given length.
3. What does *basting* mean? Learn to sew a buttonhole.
4. Could you spend a day sewing like Laura? If not, what task do you think you could do?

### Chapter 6: The Month of Roses

1. Learn about roses. Find out what roses are likely to have grown wild on the Dakota prairie. Bring in some wild roses.
2. What do you imagine are all the smells of Laura's town? What are the smells of your town?

### Chapter 7: Nine Dollars

1. Why does Laura feel that nine dollars is not enough?
2. If possible, hatch some live chicks, care for, and raise them.
3. Research what it will cost to go to college. Determine which school you like and then complete the form on page 93. On page 94, review *Little Town on the Prairie, The Hard Winter,* and *By the Shores of Silver Lake* to see how the family intends to pay for Mary's college. On the bottom of that page, brainstorm for ways you might pay for college.

   **Note to the teacher:** *For these activities, students need guidance. Show them how to find out about colleges. Take them to a large, metropolitan library to show them all the resources for finding college information and costs. Help them formulate letters of inquiry to colleges and direct them to appropriate offices. A tour of a nearby college would be beneficial.*

### Chapter 8: Fourth of July

1. Tell about your Fourth of July or other patriotic celebrations. How are they like De Smet's celebration? How are they different?
2. Research firecrackers and their dangers. How do they work?
3. Learn about Fort Ticonderoga, the Green Mountain Boys, and Daniel Boone.
4. Research the American flag in the summer of 1881. Compare it to the current flag.
5. What is a *despot*?
6. Read the Declaration of Independence. Discuss what it means.
7. Sing "My Country 'Tis of Thee." What is the melody from?
8. Laura defines what it means to be free. What do you think?
9. As a class, watch some horse races (they can be videotaped or live). Make predictions about who will win. Graph the results.
10. How fast must a person run to outrun horses?
11. Why do you think Laura disapproves of the teams racing for a five-dollar prize?
12. Eliza Jane Wilder will be the new school teacher in De Smet. She actually did teach school. To find out more about her, read *A Wilder in the West.* (See the bibliography, page 111.)

# Little Town on the Prairie (cont.)

## Chapter Discussions and Activities (cont.)

### Chapter 9: Blackbirds

1. Research Spanish needle grass, what it looks like, where it grows, and how it functions.
2. Ma says, "This earthly life is a battle." Is she right?
3. Find out about the *Godey's Lady's Book*. Color and cut out the paper doll of Mary and her college clothes, pages 95 and 96.
4. Find an illustration of a corset and read about how it works. Imagine wearing one night and day. What do you think of that?
5. Find out about blackbirds.
6. Brainstorm for the many ways to prepare and serve corn. How many can you name?

### Chapter 10: Mary Goes to College

1. Draw an illustration of Mary's trunk, according to the description.
2. Has anyone in your family ever gone away to college? How did you feel about it? How were things different for the Ingalls family than they were for you?
3. Mary's college was called the Iowa College for the Blind. Mary attended from 1881 through 1889. Today the college still stands, and it is called the Iowa Braille and Sight Saving School. Find out about it and its current course of study.
4. Describe a sunset. Laura thinks of her sunset as a king on a throne. What does your imagination tell you?
5. Clean your entire house from top to bottom. How long does it take? What is the hardest task? What is the most enjoyable? How do you feel when it is accomplished?
6. Find Vinton, Iowa, on a map.

### Chapter 11: Miss Wilder Teaches School

1. Has Nellie changed?
2. Why is Laura made so uncomfortable by being called "Miss Wilder"?

### Chapter 12: Snug for Winter

1. Read "The Lotus Eaters" and other poems by Alfred Lord Tennyson.
2. Have you ever found a gift meant for you before you were supposed to receive it? How did it feel to take away the surprise? Did you tell that you had found it, or did you keep the secret?

### Chapter 13: School Days

1. At the time of this story, girls and boys did not play together. Times have changed. Which do you think is the better way?
2. What do you think Nellie is planning?

### Chapter 14: Sent Home from School

1. What do you think of Miss Wilder's method of discipline?
2. What is a *hypocrite*?
3. What do you imagine Nellie Oleson has told Miss Wilder about Laura?
4. Pa and Ma feel that no matter what, Miss Wilder, as the teacher, must be respected. What do you think of this?

# Little Town on the Prairie *(cont.)*

## Chapter Discussions and Activities *(cont.)*

### Chapter 15: The School Board's Visit

1. Laura believes she has started the disorderliness by twice smiling at misbehavior. Is she responsible? What is the cause?
2. What are *lice?* What do they do? How does one get rid of them?
3. What does *two faced* mean?
4. Have you ever been in such disorderliness that it was disturbing to you? What happened?
5. What is meant by "A dog that will fetch a bone, will carry a bone"?

### Chapter 16: Name Cards

1. Design name cards for yourself. Use a computer program or design them freehand.
2. What is the history of your name? Why were you given it?

### Chapter 17: The Sociable

1. Color and cut out the paper dolls and clothes of Laura. (See pages 97 and 98.)
2. Construct a paper model or draw illustrations of Mrs. Tinkham's home.
3. Who is John Brown?
4. Draw an illustration of Rev. Brown as he is described by Laura in the book.
5. Have a class social like the one in the book. Serve custard and cake. Charge a dime and use that as a fundraiser for a special cause.

### Chapter 18: Literaries

1. What is a *literary society?*
2. Have a classroom spelling bee. For a challenge, invite parents and family members to join.
3. What does Laura learn about Mr. Foster? What does this suggest about judging people?

### Chapter 19: The Whirl of Gaiety

1. Host a musical program. Involve students and parents.
2. Have a potluck supper for students and their families. If desired, call it a New England supper and serve foods such as the ones in the book.
3. Have a class debate on the topic in this chapter or other topics of interest to the class.
4. In *Laura Ingalls Wilder Country* (see bibliography, page 111), you can find a sample of Mary's handwriting.
5. Practice standing like a wax figure. Who in the class can be immobile the longest?

### Chapter 20: The Birthday Party

1. Find out about the electric telegraph and how it works.
2. What is a *Quaker?* a *Quaker meeting?*
3. Practice folding cloth napkins. Can you make a flower as Mrs. Woodworth does?
4. Eat and enjoy potato pancakes. To make them, mash potatoes (page 58) and then mold the potatoes into patties. Fry the patties golden-brown on each side.
5. Play drop the handkerchief and blindman's buff.
6. Research electricity. What is it?

# Little Town on the Prairie (cont.)

## Chapter Discussions and Activities (cont.)

### Chapter 21: The Madcap Days

1. Laura and Mary Power make their own hats. Try making a hat for yourself out of whatever materials you would like.
2. Minstrel shows were once very popular. People did not look at the degrading offensiveness of their actions, doing a comical imitation of blacks. There are many reasons why they did not look at this. What do you think some of those reasons might have been?
3. Clearly, the Ingalls family sees nothing wrong with the minstrel show. For them, it is great fun. Do you think they intended anything offensive by it?
4. What do you think of the minstrel show?

### Chapter 22: Unexpected in April

1. Is Pa right, saying that one should prepare for the worst?
2. What is the strangest weather you have ever experienced?

### Chapter 23: Schooltime Begins Again

1. How does one of your summers compare with Laura's?
2. What do you think of Mr. Owen's punishment of Willie?
3. Find out about *hoops*. What did they look like? How did a lady wear them?
4. What is an *atheist?*
5. Laura is changing. What is happening to her that shows the changes in her as a young woman?
6. Find Spring Valley, Minnesota, on a map. Where is it in relation to Walnut Grove (Plum Creek)?

### Chapter 24: The School Exhibition

1. Organize and host a school exhibition in the style of the one in the book. Involve the entire school. Hold the exhibition in the evening for parents and families to attend.

### Chapter 25: Unexpected in December

1. Do you think 15 is too young to teach school?
2. Diagram sentences.
3. Laura wants to face the future bravely. How would you react in her position?

## Culminations

1. Make autograph books. Have classmates, friends, and family members sign them. (See page 99 for an autograph book cover and interior page.)
2. Have a class party like the one Ben Woodworth has. Serve the same foods and play the same games. Determine a way to experience a mild electric shock (such as by rubbing feet on the carpet and lightly touching one another).
3. Make a small-scale model of Laura's little town. Construct it from boxes, paper, cardboard, and whatever other materials you have available. Add an electric train and track.

# Going to College

You will need to do some research, including contacting your school of choice, to complete this form.

**College I Would Like to Attend:** _____

**Location:** _____

**Attendance:** _____

**Assets:** _____

_____

_____

_____

_____

**What I Would Like to Study:** _____

**Current Cost of a Four-Year Education:** _____

**Current Costs for Books and Supplies:** _____

**Current Costs for Room and Board:** _____

**Total Current Costs:** _____

(To find the projected costs, learn what the costs have been for this college over the years. Use the trend you see as the prices increase in order to project what the costs will be when you are ready to go.)

**Projected Cost of a Four-Year Education:** _____

**Projected Costs for Books and Supplies:** _____

**Projected Costs for Room and Board:** _____

**Total Projected Costs:** _____

**Why I Would Like to Attend This College:** _____

_____

_____

_____

_____

# Going to College *(cont.)*

Brainstorm for all the ways the Ingalls family has saved and plans to pay for Mary's education.

Brainstorm for all the ways you might pay for a college education. Include possible scholarships, grants, jobs, savings, and so on. You will need to research to find what financial support might be available and for what you qualify.

# Dressing Mary

Color and cut out this paper doll of Mary as she prepares for college. Color and cut out her clothes on the following page.

# Dressing Mary *(cont.)*

# Dressing Laura

Color and cut out this paper doll of Laura as she prepares for the sociable. Color and cut out her clothes on the following page.

# Dressing Laura (cont.)

# Autograph Album

Color and cut out the album cover. Duplicate as many interior pages as desired. Stack and staple the book together. Have classmates, friends, and family members write messages and autographs in the pages.

Autograph Album

# Other Books by the Author

There are several other books in print by Laura Ingalls Wilder. Below is an annotated bibliography.

*These Happy Golden Years* (1943, Harper & Row)

The eighth book in the Little House series, *These Happy Golden Years,* tells of Laura's experiences as a teacher, the completion of her own education, the growth of the Ingalls family farm, and Laura and Almanzo's courtship and marriage. It is a joyful book and an uplifting culmination to the series.

*The First Four Years* (1971, Harper & Row)

Though *These Happy Golden Years* was initially the final book in the series, a draft for *The First Four Years* was found among Laura's papers after her death. The book was originally meant to be called *The First Three Years and the Year of Grace.* It is not completely in the same style as the other books, and it is believed that Laura had begun it before Almanzo's death, but that after his death she did not wish to finish it. The book tells the story of the beginning years of the Wilders' marriage and the birth of their two children. Rose's story continues in a new series (see the bibliography, page 111). The Wilder's second child, a son, died shortly after birth. (Note: Another series predates Laura's books and tells the story of Laura's mother, Caroline, during her childhood in Wisconsin. See the bibliography.)

*On the Way Home* (1962, HarperCollins)

This book is Laura's diary account of the move she, Almanzo, and Rose took from De Smet to their new home in Missouri, "Land of the Big Red Apple." It is introduced by Rose, a respected and talented author herself. The book was published six years after Laura's death.

*West from Home: Letters of Laura Ingalls Wilder, San Francisco, 1915* (1974, Harper & Row)

This book is a collection of letters Laura sent to Almanzo while visiting their grown daughter Rose and her husband Gilette Lane in California during the world's fair of 1915. The letters give insight into the relationships between Laura and Almanzo, Laura and Rose, and even Almanzo and Rose, as well as a taste of the Panama-Pacific International Exposition and life in San Francisco early in the twentieth century.

*Little House in the Ozarks* (1991, Thomas Nelson, Inc.)

Edited by Stephen W. Hines, this book is a collection of the articles and essays Laura wrote and published before writing and publishing her books. She wrote them all from Rocky Ridge Farm, the Missouri home she and Almanzo built. The topics are varied, and collectively they certainly provide insight into the nature and character of the beloved author.

*A Little House Sampler* (1988, University of Nebraska Press)

This book is a collection of 47 poems, articles, essays, letters, and stories written by both Laura and Rose. It is written from their adult perspectives, and most of the writings predate the writing of the Little House series. A number of family photographs are also included in the book.

# Cornhusk Doll

Pioneers did not always have the means or materials for china or cloth dolls, so dolls of any available materials were made. In *Little House in the Big Woods,* we see how Laura is pleased with a corncob and handkerchief doll named Susan before she is given her beloved Charlotte.

Here are directions for a doll made from cornhusks, a type the Ingalls girls are likely to have had.

## Materials:

- scissors, yarn, crayons or marking pens, cornhusks or heavy crepe paper

## Directions:

1. Fold a cornhusk or length of crepe paper in half.
2. Tie a bit of yarn near the fold to make the neck and head.
3. Fold another shorter length.
4. Place the shorter length through the first cornhusk at right angles.
5. Tie a bit of yarn beneath it to hold it in place and to make the waist.
6. Tie a bit of yarn near the end of each arm to make the wrists and hands.
7. If making a boy doll, snip up from the bottom of the cornhusks (not quite to the waist) to make two legs. Tie bits of yarn near the bottom of the legs to make the ankles and feet. If making a girl doll, leave the husk as is for a skirt.
8. Draw on a face. Your doll is complete.

1          2          3, 4          5, 6          7

# Laura Ingalls Wilder
# Word Search

In the box are 35 names and places that are of significance in the Little House books. They can be found across, down, up, or diagonally in the puzzle. Circle them as you find them.

**Challenge:** Cover the word box to see how many you can find on your own.

| | | | | |
|---|---|---|---|---|
| Almanzo | Brewster School | Cap Garland | Caroline | Carrie |
| Charles | Dakota Territory | De Smet | Eliza Jane | Wisconsin |
| Grace | Ida Brown | Independence | Ingalls | Kansas |
| Laura | Malone | Mary | Mary Power | Minnesota |
| Missouri | Mr. Boast | Mr. Edwards | Nellie Oleson | Pepin |
| Plum Creek | Reverend Alden | Rocky Ridge | Rose | Royal |
| Silver Lake | Spring Valley | Vinton | Walnut Grove | Wilder |

```
S A L M A N Z O M R E D W A R D S W D E
P B A I P X Y Z X I D A B R O W N A A G
R D U S L R M W I L D E R O G P H L K D
I S R S U M A L O N E D E S M E T N O I
N L A O M R R S W P M L W E K P J U T R
G L T U C B Y I W K A N S A S I X T A Y
V A B R R O P L Z V I N T O N N Y G T K
A G C I E A O V D F E E E G H J G R E C
L N R Q E S W E P N N L R M L K R O R O
L I X Y K T E R I R S I S O D T A V R R
E C A P G A R L A N D Z C O Y Y C E I N
Y A H J K L O A M N O A H H P A E Q T R
L R Z M A R Y K Y X W J O V A U L T O S
B R X C A V N E L D G A O H J R K L R M
W I S C O N S I N U T N L S R Q L P Y O
V E M I N N E S O T A E W X Y Z B E D G
R E V E R E N D A L D E N Q S R R F S F
A Q A M N E L L I E O L E S O N B D P L
A K J I H P I N D E P E N D E N C E O N
```

# An Ingalls Family Motto

Beginning in the top left corner at the bolded letter T, work around the box of letters clockwise, writing down each third letter on the lines below. The letters will spell a phrase commonly spoken in the Ingalls household.

**Hint:** *You will have to go around the square almost three times to complete the phrase.*

| | | | | | | | | | | |
|---|---|---|---|---|---|---|---|---|---|---|
| **T** | T | O | H | L | M | E | O | E | R | S |
| S | | | | | | | | | | S |
| A | | | | | | | | | | E |
| N | | | | | | | | | | S |
| T | | | | | | | | | | M |
| E | | | | | | | | | | I |
| I | | | | | | | | | | W |
| U | | | | | | | | | | A |
| R | | | | | | | | | | S |
| A | O | G | G | H | O | L | T | N | L | I |

“___ ___ ___ ___ ___   ___ ___   ___ ___

___ ___ ___ ___ ___   ___ ___ ___ ___

___ ___ ___ ___ ___ ___ ___   ___ ___,”___ ___

___ ___ ___ ___ ___   ___ ___ ___ ___.”

# Culminating Activity:
# Life in the Little House

To culminate your unit on Laura Ingalls Wilder, it would be appropriate to have a festival honoring her and her books. To do so, you might choose to decorate the classroom with pictures and corresponding maps, either made by the students or acquired from the various Ingalls and Wilder homesites. (See pages 108 and 109.) You can also ask for and borrow a variety of antique pieces that might have been found in an Ingalls or Wilder home, such as quilts, butter churns, old dishes and knickknacks, old books, 19th century schoolbooks, farm tools, and so on. Serve a variety of foods from the Ingalls books. Some recipes can be found within these pages, or an excellent source for recipes is *The Little House Cookbook* by Barbara M. Walker (see bibliography, page 111). It would be particularly appropriate to serve gingerbread, for in Laura's later years she was renowned for her excellent gingerbread.

During your festival, you will likely want to listen to some fiddle music as well, live if possible, and play the only known recording of Laura's voice (see bibliography, page 111.) You can also make or find and wear pioneer clothes appropriate to the time. Then, on their own, the students might read biographies of Laura's life and compare them to her books or watch reruns of the televised series and compare the two. They can also read accounts of pioneer life told by other authors. Library shelves are filled with such stories and nonfiction books.

For an altogether different approach to culminating your unit, an industrious and enthusiastic class can build an actual classroom model of one of the Ingalls family homes. Choose a large corner of your classroom and construct a corner of the family's living area. You can make a floor, ceiling, and two walls, all from the cardboard pieces taken from large appliance boxes. The various pieces that go within the house can also be cut from cardboard. Each piece can be colored and painted, and actual cloth curtains, bedding, rag rugs, tablecloths, and so on can be made or donated. This project will take a great deal of effort, but the rewards are well worth it. When complete, invite the other classrooms and parents to have a tour, during which time you can play recordings of fiddle music, serve an Ingalls family treat, and wear pioneer costumes.

On the pages that follow (pages 105–107), you will find patterns for various items found within the Ingalls' homes. (See also the patterns on pages 48–50.) To use them, enlarge them with an overhead projector to the size desired and trace them onto butcher paper. Color, cut out, and glue the butcher paper to cardboard to make the furnishings.

# Culminating Activity:
# Life in the Little House *(cont.)*

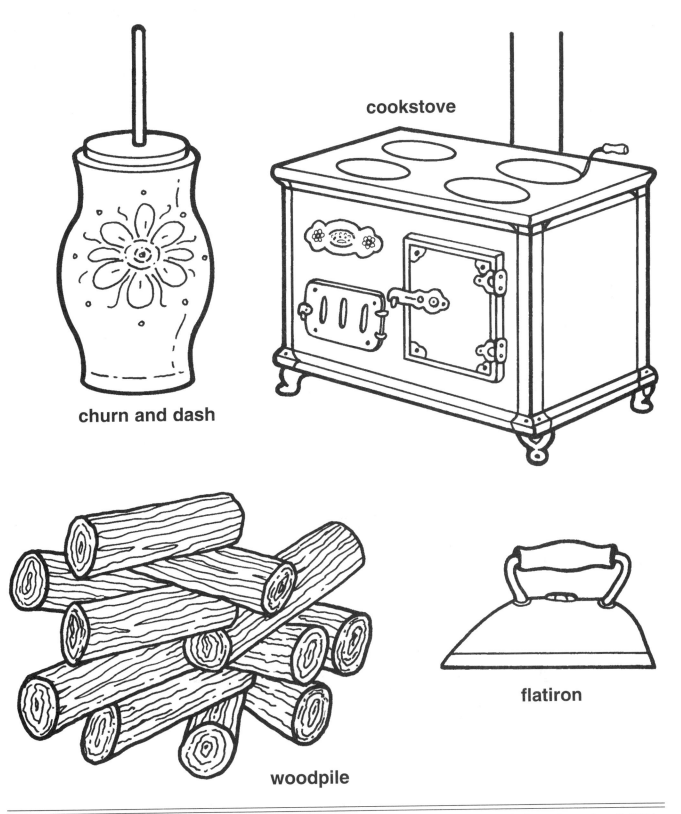

cookstove

churn and dash

woodpile

flatiron

# Culminating Activity:
# Life in the Little House *(cont.)*

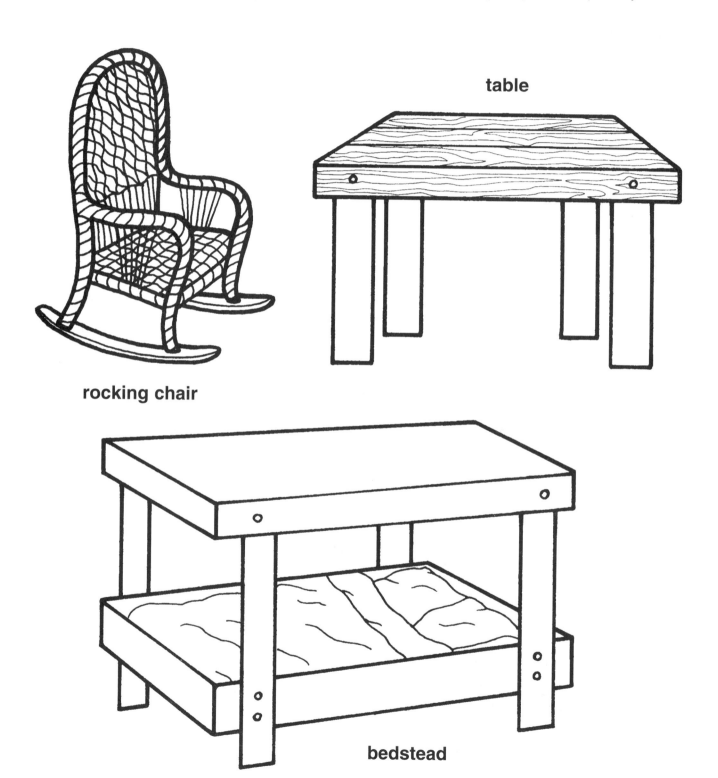

table

rocking chair

bedstead

# Culminating Activity: Life in the Little House *(cont.)*

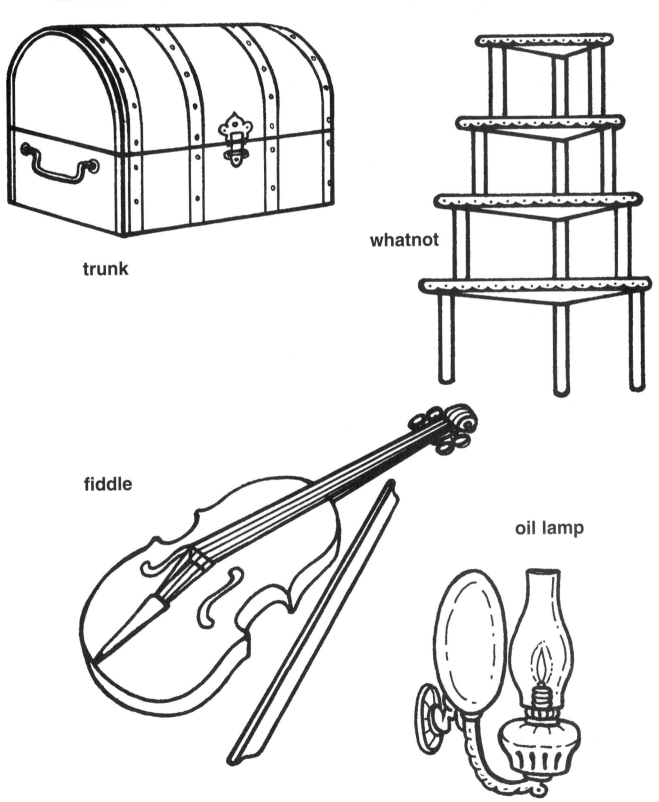

trunk

whatnot

fiddle

oil lamp

# Author Map and Locations

On page 109 is a map showing various locations in the books by Laura Ingalls Wilder. Also listed below are the homesites and the addresses to which you may write. If asking for information about the homesites, send stamped, self-addressed envelopes.

**Laura Ingalls Wilder Memorial Society, Inc.**
P.O. Box 269
Pepin, Wisconsin 54759

**Almanzo and Laura Ingalls Wilder Association**
P.O. Box 283
Malone, NY 12953

**Little House on the Prairie**
P.O. Box 110
Independence, Kansas 67301

**Laura Ingalls Wilder Museum and Tourist Center**
P.O. Box 58
Walnut Grove, Minnesota 56180

**Laura Ingalls Wilder Park and Museum**
P.O. Box 354
Burr Oak, Iowa 52131

**Laura Ingalls Wilder Site**
909 South Broadway
Spring Valley, Minnesota 55975

**Laura Ingalls Wilder Memorial Society, Inc.**
P.O. Box 344
De Smet, South Dakota 57231

**Laura Ingalls Wilder Home Association and Museum**
Route 1, Box 24
Mansfield, Missouri 65704

These first two libraries house special collections and exhibits pertaining to Laura Ingalls Wilder. The third library maintains special papers and letters by Laura Ingalls Wilder and Rose Wilder Lane. Upon request by schoolteachers, the Herbert Hoover Library will distribute a special guide concerning these papers, including excerpted letters from Laura to Rose and Rose to Laura. (It also includes samples of Laura's writing.) The library will also send copies of papers from their archives at the cost of .25 per page with a minimum charge of $6.00 for mail orders.

**Laura Ingalls Wilder Library**
Detroit, Michigan

**Pomona Public Library** (Laura Ingalls Wilder Children's Room)
Pomona, California

**Herbert Hoover Library**
West Branch, Iowa 52358

# Author Map and Locations *(cont.)*

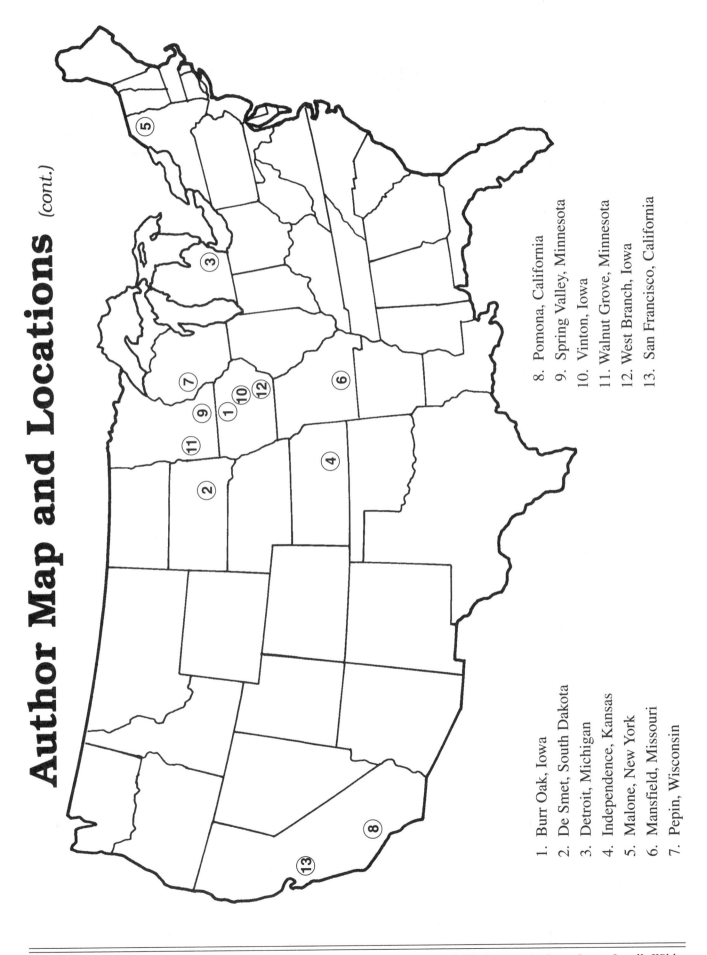

1. Burr Oak, Iowa
2. De Smet, South Dakota
3. Detroit, Michigan
4. Independence, Kansas
5. Malone, New York
6. Mansfield, Missouri
7. Pepin, Wisconsin
8. Pomona, California
9. Spring Valley, Minnesota
10. Vinton, Iowa
11. Walnut Grove, Minnesota
12. West Branch, Iowa
13. San Francisco, California

# Author Chronology

**1836** Charles Philip Ingalls is born in Cuba, New York, on January 10.

**1839** Caroline Lake Quiner is born in Milwaukee County, Wisconsin, on December 12.

**1857** Almanzo James Wilder is born near Malone, New York, on February 13.

**1860** Charles and Caroline are married in Concord, Wisconsin, on February 1.

**1865** Mary Amelia Ingalls is born in Pepin, Wisconsin, on January 10.

**1867** Laura Elizabeth Ingalls is born in Pepin on February 7.

**1869** The Ingalls family moves to Indian Territory, Kansas, near Independence.

**1870** Caroline (Carrie) Celestia is born in Montgomery County, Kansas, on August 3.

**1871** The Ingalls family moves back to their Pepin home.

**1874** The Ingalls family moves to Walnut Grove (Plum Creek), Minnesota.

**1875** Charles Frederick Ingalls is born in Walnut Grove on November 1.

**1876** Charles Frederick Ingalls dies on August 27 and is buried in South Troy, Minnesota.

**1876** The Ingalls family moves to Burr Oak, Iowa.

**1877** Grace Pearl Ingalls is born in Burr Oak on May 23.

**1878** The Ingalls family moves back to Walnut Grove, Minnesota.

**1879** The Ingalls family moves to Dakota Territory.

**1880** The town of De Smet in South Dakota is established.

**1882** Laura receives her first teaching certificate.

**1883** Laura teaches her first school.

**1885** Laura Ingalls and Almanzo Wilder are married in De Smet on August 25.

**1886** Rose Wilder is born in De Smet on December 5.

**1889** A son is born to Laura and Almanzo in August and dies within the month.

**1889** Mary graduates from the Iowa College for the Blind.

**1890** The Wilder family moves to Westville, Florida.

**1892** The Wilder family returns to De Smet.

**1894** The Wilder family moves to Mansfield, Missouri, and purchases Rocky Ridge Farm. Laura keeps a diary of the trip.

**1901** Grace Ingalls and Nate Dow (a farmer) are married in De Smet on October 16.

**1902** Charles Ingalls dies in De Smet on June 8.

**1904** Rose Wilder graduates from Crowley High School in Louisiana.

**1909** Rose Wilder marries Claire Gillette Lane in San Francisco, California, on March 24.

**1911** Laura publishes her first writing in the *Missouri Ruralist* on February 18. It is entitled, "Favors the Small Farm Home."

**1911** Rose Wilder Lane gives birth to a son, her only child, who dies.

**1912** Carrie Ingalls marries David Swanzey in Rapid City, South Dakota, on August 1. He has two children. (David Swanzey is credited with naming Mount Rushmore. The Swanzeys lived at the foot of Mount Rushmore in Keystone, South Dakota.)

**1912** Laura becomes a columnist and the Home Editor for the *Missouri Ruralist*.

**1915** Laura visits Rose in San Francisco, California, for the world's fair. While there, she publishes poems in the *San Francisco Bulletin*.

**1918** Rose and Gillette Lane are divorced.

**1919** In June, Laura publishes an article in *McCall's* entitled, "The Farmer's Wife Says."

**1923** Laura discontinues her work for the *Missouri Ruralist*.

**1924** Caroline Ingalls dies in De Smet on April 20.

**1925** On January 17, Laura publishes an article in the *Country Gentleman* entitled, "My Ozark Kitchen."

**1928** Mary Ingalls dies in Keystone, South Dakota, on October 17.

**1932** *Little House in the Big Woods* is published.

**1933** *Farmer Boy* is published.

**1935** *Little House on the Prairie* is published.

**1937** *On the Banks of Plum Creek* is published.

**1938** Laura and Almanzo take a holiday to the Pacific Coast.

**1938** *On the Banks of Plum Creek* is named a Newbery Honor Book.

**1939** *By the Shores of Silver Lake* is published.

**1940** *By the Shores of Silver Lake* is named a Newbery Honor Book.

**1940** *The Long Winter* is published.

**1941** *The Long Winter* is named a Newbery Honor Book.

**1941** Grace Ingalls Dow dies in Manchester, South Dakota, on November 10.

**1941** *Little Town on the Prairie* is published.

**1942** *By the Shores of Silver Lake* is awarded the Pacific Northwest Library Young Reader's Choice Award.

**1942** *Little Town on the Prairie* is named a Newbery Honor Book.

**1943** *These Happy Golden Years* is published.

**1944** *These Happy Golden Years* is named a Newbery Honor Book.

**1946** Carrie Ingalls Swanzey dies in Rapid City, South Dakota, on June 2.

**1949** Almanzo Wilder dies at Rocky Ridge Farm on October 23.

**1953** The Little House series is reissued with illustrations by Garth Williams. Mr. Williams does extensive research, travel, and communication with the author to authenticate the work.

**1954** The Laura Ingalls Wilder Award is established by the American Library Association. Laura herself is the first recipient.

**1957** Laura Ingalls Wilder dies at Rocky Ridge Farm on February 10.

**1962** *On the Way Home* is published.

**1968** Rose Wilder Lane dies in Danbury, Connecticut, on October 30.

**1971** *The First Four Years* is published.

**1971** The Little House books are published in paperback.

**1974** *West from Home* is published.

**1974** The television show, *Little House on the Prairie*, first airs. It runs until 1983.

**1988** *A Little House Sampler* is published.

**1991** *Little House in the Ozarks* is published.

# Bibliography and Resources

Anderson, William. *A Biography: Laura Ingalls Wilder.* HarperCollins, 1992.

_____. *Laura Ingalls Wilder Country.* HarperCollins, 1990.

_____. *Laura's Rose: The Story of Rose Wilder Lane.* (Order from the Laura Ingalls Wilder Memorial Society, Inc.)

_____. *Little House Country: A Photo Guide to the Home Sites of Laura Ingalls Wilder.* Anderson MI, 1989.

_____. *Musical Memories of Laura Ingalls Wilder.* Hear and Learn Publications, 1992; 206-694-0034.

_____. *The Story of the Ingalls: What Happened Next to Laura's Family.* (Order from the Laura Ingalls Wilder Memorial Society, Inc.)

_____. *The Story of the Wilders: What Happened Next to Almanzo's Family.* (Order from the Laura Ingalls Wilder Memorial Society, Inc.)

_____. A *Wilder in the West.* Reynolds Printing Company, 1971.

Blair, Gwenda. *Laura Ingalls Wilder.* Putnam, 1981.

Garson, Eugenia. *The Laura Ingalls Wilder Songbook.* HarperCollins, 1968.

Giff, Patricia R. *Laura Ingalls Wilder: Growing Up in the Little House.* Viking, 1987.

Greene, Carol. *Laura Ingalls Wilder: Author of the Little House Books.* Childrens Press, 1990.

_____. *The Horn Book,* December 1953. (This is a special Wilder issue.)

Lasky, Kathryn and Meribah Knight. *Searching for Laura Ingalls: A Reader's Journey.* S & S Childrens, 1993.

MacBride, Roger Lea. *In the Land of the Big Red Apple.* HarperCollins, 1995.

_____. *Little Farm in the Ozarks.* HarperCollins, 1994.

_____. *Little House on Rocky Ridge.* HarperCollins, 1993.

_____. *On the Other Side of the Hill.* HarperCollins, 1995. (This series is still expanding.)

Stine, Megan. *Laura Ingalls Wilder, Pioneer Girl.* Dell, 1992.

Walker, Barbara M. *The Little House Cookbook.* Harper & Row, 1979.

Wilkes, Maria D. *Little House in Brookfield.* HarperCollins, 1996. (part of a series)

Zochert, Donald. *Laura: The Life of Laura Ingalls Wilder.* Avon, 1976.

## Resources

**The Ashton-Drake Galleries** has manufactured a set of dolls from the series, including Laura, Mary, Almanzo, and Nellie. Write them at 9200 North Maryland Avenue, Niles, Illinois 60714-1397 or call them at 1-800-346-2460.

*The De Smet News* **in De Smet, South Dakota**, offers packets of reprints and postcards for $2.25. The packet contains information that supports the authenticity of the characters and the stories.

**Harper & Row**, the publishers of the Little House books, may provide book jackets and promotional displays. Write to them at 10 East 53rd Street, New York, NY 10022.

**Laura Ingalls Wilder Speaks**, the only known recording of her voice, may be purchased from The Laura Ingalls Wilder Home Association. Call them at (417) 924-3626 or see the address on page 108.

**The United States Postal Service** prints a 29 cent stamp honoring *Little House on the Prairie.*

# Answer Key

## Page 72: Time-Checks

1. pay = $10.50
2. pay = $15.75
3. pay = $24.52
4. pay = $16.14
5. pay = $13.13
6. pay = $18.02
7. pay = $9.77
8. pay = $16.73
9. pay = $31.39
10. pay = $32.33

## Page 102: Laura Ingalls Wilder Word Search

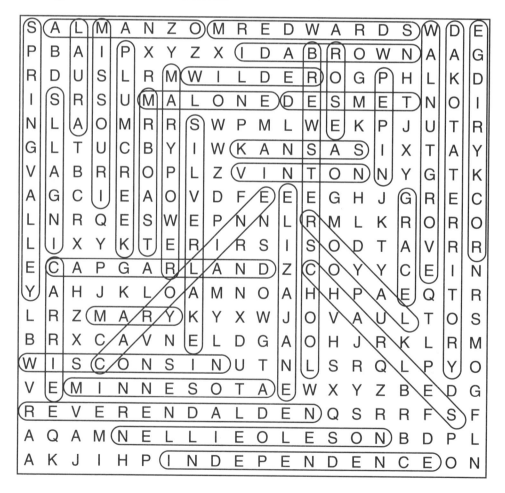

## Page 103: An Ingalls Family Motto

"There is no great loss without some small gain."